CODEPENDENCY NO MORE

*A Practical Guide to Get Rid of Codependent
Behavior, Cultivate Healthy Relationships,
and Lead A life of Freedom and Joy*

Nick Anderson

Table of Contents

Introduction 3

Chapter 1: What is Codependency Anyway? 8

Chapter 2: Is Codependency a Personality Disorder? 22

Chapter 3: Let's Begin at the Start: How Codependency Develops 40

Chapter 4: Why Do People Get Stuck in Codependent Relationships? 48

Chapter 5: Overcoming Codependency: 6 Techniques 62

Chapter 6: Admit That You Are a Codependent .. 68

Chapter 7: Assert Your Personal Boundaries 78

Chapter 8: Prioritize Self Care 94

Chapter 9: Practice Self-Compassion 103

Chapter 10: Build a Strong Support System 116

Chapter 11: Seek Professional Help 125

Conclusion 128

Introduction

I remember meeting Maria when I was in college. I was a sophomore then and she was a freshman. She just started and we met at a freshman orientation. I was there as one of a few sophomore guides for the incoming class.

We hit it off pretty well and, before you know it, we pretty much spent all our time together. It's as if I couldn't take one step in front of the other without Maria being there. She was my oxygen. It seems that whatever life had to offer, it only had meaning because my girlfriend was there with me.

Little did I know that early on in college, I was developing a codependent mindset. It took me several years to realize just how much damage codependency has on both my maturity as a human being and my effectiveness as a sentient, caring, and compassionate person.

The problem with codependency that many Americans have is that we place a very high value on relationships. We think that our relationships have to define us. We walk on eggshells regarding how we deal with other people because we don't want them to say an unkind word. We don't want them to change how they look at us.

Before we know it, we become slaves to other people's perceptions and we're no longer autonomous, strong, mature individuals. It's as if we live our lives based on other people's approval.

This also goes the other way and this is what establishes the codependency "loop." When you feel that everything you do has to please another person or live up to their standards or expectations, it's only a matter of time until you demand the same from them. You may be thinking that this is just a healthy way of developing reciprocity in your relationship. You might even fool yourself into thinking that this is a way where you and your lover or romantic partner or your family member can "grow together."

Those are lies. Seriously. What you're in is a codependent relationship that goes only one way. That's right. You create a downward spiral and before you know it, none of you are growing. None of you are moving forward and guess what? You become even more toxic to future people who enter your life.

I know that this sounds depressing or even discouraging but this is what has been my experience with Maria and other relationships after her. Until I was able to break free of the gravitational pull of codependent relationship patterns, I was unable to mature as a human being. In other words, I was unable to become fully independent on an emotional, intellectual, and definitely spiritual level.

This book is dedicated to people who are in codependent relationships whether they know it or not. Whether you can see the symptoms of codependency in your relationship or you know for a fact that you are in a codependent situation, this book can help you break free.

Please understand that the only person getting in the way of your maturity and happiness is you. Not your parents, not the traumatic situations that may have happened in your past, not what other people say about you, but you. You have to take the initiative. You can't spend the rest of your life blaming an ex-girlfriend, ex-boyfriend, ex-husband, or ex-wife.

You have to get out from the gravitational pull of your past regardless of whatever emotional or sexual abuse you may have experienced. The past is the past. It's not like you have a time machine you can jump into and somehow change those facts. Those facts happened.

Your job is to become an adult and look those facts the way they need to be looked at. You need to treat them the way they need to be treated. Let me give you a spoiler. Those past facts should not run your life. Those past facts should not limit you as far as your potential is concerned, much less make you miserable in the here and now.

Can you imagine how pointlessness this is where you allow yourself to feel depressed or anxious or guilty about things the happened in the past? They already happened. Let them go.

You can choose a new relationship and a new attitude towards your past today. Those facts are not going to go away but your mindset regarding them can change. By taking responsibility over this choice, you become more resistant to codependency. You also develop a mindset where you're more likely to identify potential codependency factors before things get hot and ultimately get desperate.

A lot of people approach codependency much like a person stepping into a quicksand. I don't know about you but it's very easy to get into a quicksand. You're walking along and then there are some patches of some sandy dirt and, at first, it feels like mud. You don't think much about it. It's like the kind of watery mess that you have waded into before. You stick your feet in and you assume that you'll be able to keep walking and go on your way.

Obviously, this is not the case because you stepped into a quicksand. Just because you didn't recognize at first doesn't make the danger go away and then when you treat it like it is normal, you end up making things worse for yourself.

This is how codependency works. When you know that you have a pattern of codependency but you hope against hope that somehow someway this relationship is going to be different, you're not doing yourself any favors. It's time to be an adult and to assume that you are part of a pattern, and for you to enjoy the best that life has to offer, you have to step up and be proactive regarding the relationships you get into or you choose to maintain.

Please understand that this book on codependency is not just about romantic relationships. This is also about your relationship to your parents, to your friends, or even your boss. So, dig in and it's going to be a wild ride because we're going to explore the key issues involving codependency and how you can get out from under them.

Chapter 1: What is Codependency Anyway?

It's very easy to criticize the concept of codependency as strictly an American phenomenon. It's very easy for people who come from other cultural backgrounds to say, "Well, codependency is only an issue if you grew up in the west or you have some sort of European orientation." After all, compared to people from eastern cultures, western people tend to be more autonomous, independent, and individual-centered.

Asians, generally speaking, define their identity in terms of family or some larger social unit. For example in Northeast Asia, in particular I'm talking about South Korea and Japan as well as certain parts of China, a person is not necessarily defined as an individual.

Instead, that person is always part of a larger identity involving family surname, ethnolinguistic regional group, or trade association, professional association, even religious sect. In other words, the idea of individualism is always subsumed within a larger social reality. And it's this social reality that gives meaning to the individuals within that group.

It's easy to see within this contrast that codependency may be defined as strictly an

American or western problem. Here's the problem with that excuse and I call it by its name. It's an excuse. You don't necessarily have to live in Los Angeles, San Francisco, New York or Tampa, Florida, to feel the negative effects of codependency.

Codependency is codependency whether you live in Manila, Mumbai, Dubai, or Kinshasa, Africa. Codependency hurts. It robs people of their full potential. It doesn't matter what color skin they have. It doesn't matter what religion they're into. It doesn't matter what job they have or how much money they have in the bank.

Codependency has a way of robbing you of your ability to love and demand love, to respect and expect respect to such a point that you become an empty hull. Your relationships are no longer driven by mutual happiness and mutual desire for something better. Instead, it's driven by fear. You feel like you're always settling. You feel like you're always walking on eggshells.

In fact, if you take it to its furthest logical extreme, this is not much of a relationship. It is emotional slavery. That may be frank. If you're in a codependent relationship, you are not doing yourself any favors. Stop making excuses as to culture and background. Codependency will always be codependency regardless of where it is and when it happens.

What is Codependency?

Codependency was first diagnosed by psychiatrists and psychologists in the 1970s when they studied alcoholism. They noticed that when people were trying to break free of alcoholism, somehow very important members of their family (normally their wives) ended up playing a big role in the recovery process.

This role is not always positive. In many cases, family members engaged in behaviors that made it likely, less likely, or more likely for the alcoholic or drug addict to continue their behavior. In other words, when somebody is trying to overcome alcoholism or substance addiction, their social context in terms of their close relationships have a big role to play in how easy or how difficult it is to break free of that addiction.

The researchers, in particular, found behavior patterns by spouses and family members that actually enabled alcoholics and addicts to persist in their behavior. Of course, when you ask these people, they don't want their family member to remain an addict or an alcoholic but when you pay close attention to what they did and how they interacted with their family member, it produced an opposite result.

The first paper on codependency was released around 1970 and it involved alcoholics. By zeroing in on enabling behavior by close family members and spouses, searchers found that these people, although they are not addicted to alcoholic drinks, can be safely defined as co-alcoholics. In other words, they may not be struggling with addiction themselves but they had psychological issues that made it hard for the alcoholic or the drug abuser to break their addiction.

Typical Codependency Behaviors

Upon examining the codependent and family members, the researchers saw that these people were motivated by noble intentions. They truly wanted their addicted partners and family members to quit. That wasn't the problem. The issue is the way they tried to "pick up the pieces" or rescue or "fix" their partner, the worse the problem got or the more likely the addict or alcoholic would remain in addiction.

Extending the Pattern

Codependent relationship patterns have been observed by psychological researchers to extend beyond drug addiction and alcoholism. In fact, by the mid-1980s, researchers reported that codependency factors also applied to gambling addicts, shopaholics, workaholics, and sex addicts. At this point, the previously dominant label of "co-alcoholic" gave way to the more accurate "codependent."

Codependency Means Both Partners Have Issues

When you're in a codependent relationship, it's very easy to look at the problems of your partner. Maybe they're addicted to gambling, shopping, work, sex, drugs, alcohol, and it's easy to define yourself as free of all that. But in turns out, according to psychotherapists, you also have issues of your own. The fact that you try to "save" your partner according to some sort of selfish agenda is a manifestation of this dysfunctional compulsion.

You may not be addicted to the same things but the same process applies to you and because you're unaware of this, it becomes harder for your partner to break free of whatever issue he or she is struggling with.

Codependency Problems Don't Just Stem from the "Problem Partner"

A lot of the early research regarding codependency turned on whether the dysfunction exhibited by the non-alcoholic or non-addict partner stemmed from the relationship. In other words, the researchers asked, "But for the other partner being an addict would this other partner have such psychological issues?"

The answer, it turned out, was no. The problem didn't begin with the problematic partner. It turns out that a lot of people who find themselves in codependent relationships have a history of such relationships.

It's not unusual for a person to first hook up with an alcoholic and then when that relationship falls apart, she then moves on to a drug addict and then to a gambling addict and so on and so forth. The issue is she has this pattern of relating to other people who corrode and degrade the quality of a relationship.

When you ask people who are in serial codependent relationships, they often describe themselves as simply unlock or victims. They look at themselves as completely free of any contribution or responsibility for what's happening to their other partner. They look at themselves as the knight in shining armor or the person who's just trying to help. They rarely look at themselves as being part the problem.

The truth is after several psychological studies on this issue, a clear pattern emerged. There is such a thing as relationship addiction and it has a strong correlation with the brain chemicals released in alcoholics and substance abusers.

The Core Component of Codependency

Given that codependency plays out in different types of relationships involving different kinds of negative behaviors or addictions to dismiss it as a purely situation-based mental state. After extensive psychological meta-studies of many independent studies of codependent relationships conducted over many years, researchers were able to identify a key psychological concept that defines codependency.

It refers to individuals that become very emotionally and intellectually dependent on certain people in their lives and they end up feeling that they are responsible for these other people and these people are responsible for their own happiness and self-worth. In other words, they define themselves based solely on what this other person thinks or feels. They are both in a very dependent and somewhat aggressive position.

The Risk of Codependency

What's so bad about being codependent?

If you didn't read the pervious section, it's very easy to forgive you for asking this question. When you are dependent fully on somebody else's approval, validation, and emotional support, you are no longer your own person. Before you know it, you decide everything that you based on not what you think is right or what is sensible or based on your own person experience and logic.

Instead, you're always looking at emotional factors. Last time I checked, emotion and logic don't always line up. In fact, in many cases, they are completely opposite of each other and lead to different paths and different outcomes. It would be great if we lived in a fully logical reasonable world but you know and I know that's not the case. Emotion does play a big role.

However, the problem here is not necessarily your emotions but other people's emotions. You are so dependent on their validation, approval, and support that you base your life almost solely on their input. This makes you very easy to manipulate. It can also make you a manipulator. You are at risk of being a codependent if the following factors are present in your life.

You have a Partner or a Close Friend or Family Member Who Engages in Addictive or Compulsive Behavior or Abuses Substances

Keep in mind that this is a broad definition. It's easy to think that if somebody is an alcoholic or a drug addict, then that's the only person you should avoid when it comes to codependency. The lines are not that clearly drawn because the key here is not so much what they are addicted to but their compulsive behavior.

You have to understand that people get addicted to so many things. There are video game addicts, shopping addicts, workaholics, relationship addicts, gossip addicts, you name it.

How do you make heads or tails of all these different permutations and variations? Very simple. If they can't help themselves or they feel that they have to do something first before doing something else, then chances are they are expressing addictive behavior.

If you are in a relationship with that person or you are in close contact or exposure to that person on a day-to-day basis, you have a higher chance of developing codependency. This can be a family member. This can be your brother or sister. This can be a parent. You don't necessarily have to be in a romantic relationship with this person.

You are in a Dependent Position to Somebody Suffering from Compulsive Behavior

You are in an emotionally dependent position to somebody suffering from compulsive behavior. If you are and adult and your parent is an alcoholic, this can definitely apply to you.

However, as I mentioned above, there are many variations to these. Maybe your parent is a gambling addict. Perhaps that person is just glued to video games all day every day. Possibly, that person is addicted to Facebook and is just always thrown off by notifications, whether people liked or didn't like, or whether people left comments or not.

The key here is not to focus on the substance that the person is addicted to but on the behavior of that person. If it seems that this adult can't seem to live without a certain stimulation from a particular source, maybe it's virtual, perhaps it's a physical chemical substance, or possibly it's other people, then chances are you are dealing with an addict at some level or other.

You Grew Up in an Environment that was Chaotic due to Addiction or Mental Impairment

Codependency can also arise in persons who grew up in family situations where at least one parent is irresponsible. Maybe this person's ability to care for his or his or her family was impaired by alcoholism or drug addiction. In many situations, this impairment can also come from different sources like your mother, for example, was a victim of child sex abuse or your father was abandoned by his own father early on and he grew up to be an angry person.

Whatever the case may be, when you grow up in a household where at least one parent has some sort of issue from either the past or is suffering from anxieties about the future that get in the way of them giving their children the warmth, acceptance, and love they deserve, you may be at risk of becoming a codependent .

Codependency's Most Common Manifestations

Generally speaking, codependency can happen in a range of circumstances with varying severity because let's face it relationships differ from case to case because they are made up of different people and if you combine these people and mix and match them together, the form of codependency can be quite diverse indeed.

With that said, codependency often manifests itself in a stressful family life. For example, if you're a mother who is suffering from schizophrenia or depression, it's going to put a tremendous toll on the people around you. Similarly, if your brother has some addiction to stealing, that's going to be a problem as well or if your father can't stop lying, that can be an issue.

However, in terms of the most common cause of stress, this is usually involving three things: physical illness, drug or alcohol addiction, or mental illness.

What Types of Relationships can become codependent?

If you've watched a lot of Hollywood movies, it's very easy to conclude that codependency almost always happens in a romantic relationship. We're talking about girlfriend-boyfriend, boyfriend-boyfriend, girlfriend-girlfriend, or spouses.

However, according to research, codependent relationships are actually broader than what we commonly expect. You can become codependent with a friend just as much as you can be stuck in such a relationship with romantic partners or relatives.

Codependency is Asymmetric

Asymmetric is a fancy term for unevenness. A codependent relationship involves an uneven distribution of attention, care, and emotional energy. Usually, in a codependent relationship, the addict or the person suffering from depression, anxiety or other mental and personal issues take up a lot of the emotional energy.

There's a lopsided arrangement. It's as if there is a responsible partner who seems to have gotten her act together and then there's the irresponsible partner who just is a black hole of forgiveness, understanding, and is showered with chance after chance.

Again, this doesn't have to be a romantic partner. It could be a younger brother who is very irresponsible. It could be a mother who just is caught up in depression due to a past trauma.

The Manifestations of Codependency

Now that we understand the broad outlines of how codependent relationships work and operate, let's gets to the bottom line. What is in overcoming codependency for you? In other words, how do you benefit when you break free of codependency?

In a 1990 study published in the Journal of Psychiatry, the meta-study of many other individual studies indicated that when women, in particular, break free of codefendant relationships, they let go of the heaviness they feel when they think they are responsible for the happiness of one other person in their life.

They feel free. They feel the freedom of a mature, responsible adult because they no longer feel that they have to watch what they say constantly and somehow channel emotional energy to this person who seems to just take, take, and take without giving anything back. According to researchers, this leads to letting go of the feeling of helplessness, anguish, and pain.

It's very easy to see this scenario play out when you are living with a parent suffering from Alzheimer's or who has a serious personality issue. There are many older women, these are mothers who cannot give their children praise. There's always a negative. They're always judging. They choose their words carefully so you don't really know whether they fully approve or they are simply holding back condemnation.

According to the study, when women are freed from this codependency, they start living their lives because they're no longer within the gravitational pull of the psychological hang-up of the parent they love so much. As much as most people love their mothers, they have to move on and become independent emotional adults themselves.

When they are stuck in a codependent relationship, they become perpetual children. They have the bodies of adults and the earning capacity of mature, responsible adults; they have their own cars; they have their own houses but, deep down inside, they remain kids.

According to the codependency literature starting in the 1970s, the decision to break free from such emotional arrangements leads to renewed sense of freedom, potential, and personal happiness.

Chapter 2: Is Codependency a Personality Disorder?

Now that we have a clear understanding of what codependency is and the situations it applies to, the next step is to categorize it.

It's something to think that if you are a codependent person and you can't help but get into one codependent relationship after another, that you have a certain personality disorder. Maybe this quirk is just part of a personality defect.

Well, according to the DSM psychology "bible," the Diagnostic and Statistical Manual for Mental Disorders - DSM 5, codependency is still not widely recognized as a personality issue.

There have been many arguments that say that this is a personality disorder and that it should be treated as such. But for whatever reason, the argument has always been declined.

The reason why some psychologists are saying that codependency should become part of the DSM as a specific personality disorder in and of itself, lies in its overlaps with recognized personality problems.

For example, codependency, classically defined, has elements that touch on or completely overlap borderline personality disorder as well as dependent personality disorder. Since these issues are already present in codependency, some researchers are saying that this warrants giving a specific designation for this type of personality and emotional problem.

On the other hand, other researchers say that since there is all this overlap already, there is really no need to delineate a specific disorder for codependency. It can be treated within its current relationship to other recognized personality disorders like borderline personality disorder as well as dependent personality disorder.

The argument falls apart when it comes to at least one actual research study involving codependency symptoms. According to this in-depth research, while some codependent people do have symptoms of borderline personality disorder as well as dependent personality disorder, many others who don't have these symptoms yet they exhibit all the symptoms of codependency.

This study suggests that codependency should be defined as independent and distinct from dependent personality disorder.

DPD, strictly defined, describes people who are dependent on others in general. In other words, when a person has DPD, that person will quickly become dependent on other people regardless of what prior relationship they had, regardless of the situation. That's just the way they are. They become dependent easily. It's a generalized form of dependency.

Codependent individuals, however, become dependent only on specific people within a specific type of relationship. This is what sets codependency apart from DPD.

Similarly, the analysis on BPD, or borderline personality disorder, exhibits the same logical weakness when it comes to subsuming codependent personality to BPD.

BPD relates to general instability with interpersonal relationships. People with borderline personality disorder just have problems getting along with others. This doesn't necessarily mean that they're dependent on other people.

While codependency creates a lot of negative emotional states and is a problem in and of itself, this is just a subset of the generalized interpersonal problems people with BPD have.

So, it can't be safely assumed that just because there are some overlaps with BPD that codependency is one and the same as BPD. In certain circumstances, BPD is broader because codependency is so specific.

Codependency in Relationship with Interdependence

One of the best ways to define a personality disorder or emotional or mental disorder is through comparisons.

It's one thing to say that a person is suffering from a certain condition, and then come up with a list defining that condition. But it's usually more helpful to compare that set of conditions with others who exhibit a healthier set of conditions.

In other words, one effective way of defining codependency is to define what it's not.

So, what is missing when you are in a codependent relationship? How do we determine what codependency is in comparison to a normal healthy relationship?

Here are just some things that are missing or are seriously compromised in a codependent relationship:

Each Partner has Total Freedom of Choice

When you're in a codependent relationship, you feel that you are possessed by the other person or you have a right to possession of the other person.

This ends up putting the other person under a lot of pressure. They feel that they have to guard their emotions. They can't just say something off the top of their heads because it may throw you off.

You know you're in a healthy interdependent relationship when there's enough space between you two for you to say what you want to say and say what you mean.

You don't have to worry that this person will take it the wrong way and hold it against you and feel betrayed and sad or even depressed. You don't feel that you're under such a heavy responsibility for this person's emotional state. The relationship is big enough and mature enough to allow for this frank and blunt exchange.

Codependent Relationships Involve Intertwined Identities

You know you're in a codependent relationship when your definition of who you are is closely associated with the identity of your partner. So, you start defining yourself as "I am x's girlfriend," "husband," or "spouse."

It's as if you don't have your own achievements, background, potential and skill set. It's as if your whole value necessarily turns on whatever value your partner or family member brings to the table.

This is especially true in codependent relationships involving a particularly accomplished individual. Maybe this person is very rich, or very politically substantial.

Their children would always say, "I'm the child of Senator X." It's as if their whole identity and value as human beings turn on their relationship to that other person.

Healthy interdependent relationships define each partner independently. This means that they have their own personality and opinion, and both partners agree that each of them are equally worthy of appreciation and respect.

They don't define each other based on the achievements of the other. Instead, they have their own value independent of each other and they respect each other because of that. This means there's no ranking.

In other words, it's easy for the wealthier partner to say, "You can only feel pride with that BMW I gave you." Meaning, "everything comes from me and my money." That is codependency.

An interdependent relationship means you don't care about the value that you give to the other partner. You care more about the relationship.

And each partner in the relationship has a right to use the assets of that relationship. Their use of assets in the relationship doesn't make them dependent or lower in position.

Codependent Relationships Draw Their Strength from One of the Partners

You know you're in a codependent relationship when you feel that the other person (or you) have the upper hand in the relationship. In other words, this is the definition of the strength of the relationship. It has to come from either one of you, but it has to come from one.

The idea that both of you are equally strong or have something of value to bring to the relationship is completely foreign.

You start thinking of your relationship as something valuable because your partner has money or is particularly good-looking or is desired by other people. You then subsume your strength in the relationship or your ability to make demands in it to that of your partner. That is a codependent relationship.

And interdependent relationship acknowledges the strength of both individuals. That both of you have your strong and weak points. Both of you have something to say. Both of you are equally worthy.

Accordingly, both of you respect each other's input. You don't automatically say that since your partner is a lawyer that any kind of logical decision necessarily has to be his specialty and you will just focus on something else.

Codependent Relationships are Emotionally Volatile

You know you're in a mature interdependent relationship when the intensity level of emotions in your relation with the other person remains fairly constant.

There are fluctuations because there are, of course, times where it's perfectly appropriate to feel angry, upset or shocked or fearful, but they are predictable and they are consistent. Not so with codependent relationships.

A lot of people get addicted to the highs and lows because when things get really heated and emotions are flaring up, this makes for a nasty breakup and the other partner almost always comes back.

Maybe she got battered or beaten up, but she keeps coming back because when they make up, the sense of wholeness, love, acceptance and healing she gets more than makes up for the massive crash and intensity of the breakup.

This is very dangerous. A lot of women who end up being battered to death in abusive relationships where addicted to this pattern. A classic symptom of codependent relationships.

Healthy Relationships Acknowledge a Wide Support System

You know you're in a codependent relationship when your partner says to you that you can only rely on her. In other words, she expects you to shut out your family members.

When it comes to emotional sustenance and support, you are supposed to only rely on her. Otherwise, she would feel that you don't love her. Otherwise, she would feel that you're betraying her or you don't give her the kind of respect and value she deserves. There's an emotional blackmail there and the monopolization of emotional support.

Interdependent relationships recognize that people can draw emotional support from many different places. This means you can lean your head on the shoulders of your mother and father and your partner wouldn't hold it against you. In fact, she would welcome it.

Similarly, she would allow you to have friends who could give you the support that you're looking for.

You know you're in a codependent relationship when your partner insists that you only get support from one source and one source alone: your partner.

This emotionally retards your growth. It also makes the relationship even more twisted and sick because by monopolizing and taking up the sole ability to give you the support you need, your partner has you by the neck. He or she can control you.

It only takes a word from that person for you to feel small, insignificant, defeated, humiliated and embarrassed. That's a sick relationship.

Codependent Relationships are Very Dependent on Mood

You know you're in a committed healthy relationship when your ability to treat your partner well doesn't depend on what you're feeling. You may have had a bad day, there may have been all sorts of tragedies that happened, but you can be counted on to treat your partner just right.

Codependent relationships are marked by extreme dependence on mood. Your ability to treat your partner right depends on your mood, and most importantly, on his or her mood.

You end up in a relationship that is very reactive. In other words, you're always looking for cues or signals from the other person to determine how you'll treat the other person. This obviously creates a downward spiral.

What if one or both of you woke up on the wrong side of the bed? It doesn't take a rocket scientist to figure out that this can lead to her giving you bad signals and you returning the favor. And it gets worse as she bounces off those negative signals, and you treat each other worse and worse, and guess what? Both of you are in a foul mood and the relationship becomes far more painful that it needs to be.

On the other hand, it can also work the other way. She's in a good mood, which lifts up your mood, which lifts her up even further, and so on and so forth. But given how volatile moods can be, it's not something you want to build your relationship on.

You don't know the next time you'll feel good. You don't know what circumstances you'll be in beforehand, so why allow yourself to be dependent on those things that you cannot control?

Interdependent relationships involve commitment. So regardless of what you're feeling, you commit to giving your partner the empathy or sympathy he or she deserves. You do this without necessarily making the problem your own or taking on the pain.

Instead, by choosing to be emotionally dependent, you give them the push that they need to get out of that mood or to survive that mood. Also, you're not dependent on your own mood.

Codependent Relationships Cannot Withstand Criticism or Any Kind of Evaluation

You know you're in a codependent relationship when your partner feels that you are always judging him or her.

It's as if anything negative is held against you. You can't even tell the truth. You can't say what you objectively observe because you're afraid it's going to hurt his or her feelings.

Your partner makes it abundantly clear that criticism and evaluation is off limits in your relationship. And if they keep this up, pretty soon, you expect the same from them.

It is no surprise that codependent relationships often thrive on lies. It's as if everybody else in the world could see what's going on in your relationship but both you and your partner can't seem to wake up to that reality because too much is at stake.

You don't want that person to leave you, so you lie to that person and they return the favor to you. Not exactly the definition of a healthy relationship.

Interdependent relationships, on the other hand, are built on honesty.

Let's get one thing clear: the truth hurts. But the good news about the truth is that, as much as it hurts, the pain can help you grow. You don't want to hear it, you don't want to see it, you don't want to be told, but you are mature enough to accept it and use it to grow.

It doesn't happen overnight, but when you are in a relationship where truth is welcomed, you become a more mature and balanced person. You don't waste precious time and energy trying to draw artificial lines regarding what kind of truth is welcome in your relationship.

This is crucial because if you are addicted to drugs, are an alcoholic, or a sex addict, or a victim of child sex abuse, you need to know the truth. It's not welcome, it doesn't feel good, but before you know it, you start benefitting from it because you become a better person. You start to heal. You start to resolve things.

But if you are in a relationship where you set up rules where certain truths cannot be said, then you end up enabling these negative patterns.

Your partner may be a drug addict, guess what? He or she will continue to be a drug addict. If you are addicted to sex, guess what? You will continue to be dependent. The same applies to child abuse and mental conditions.

Your relationship, instead of being a place of healing, maturity, and responsibility, becomes a pit of sickness because you allowed it to.

It's kind of like, the reality is out there, but your relationship is here and it maintains all the comforting lies that you choose to believe in, and guess what? Lies will not make you better. They will not make your problems go away. They will not help you mature into an adult.

Codependency and Substance Abuse

The last few paragraphs of the section above is a good segue to the most crushing negative effects of codependency, which is its relationship to substance abuse.

Codependency and some sort of substance abuse are intricately connected. It's as if they are two intricate ropes tied together and it's really hard to unravel that mess. Maybe the knot is too tight, or maybe the fibers are just too interwoven.

Whatever the case may be, and whatever the substance abuse may involve, you need to pay attention to how codependency works in this situation.

Let's get one thing clear, being addicted to any kind of chemical substance is bad enough in and of itself. Did you know that nicotine is more addicting than heroin? Maybe you or your partner is addicted to alcohol. Well, these are weighty problems in and of themselves, but when codependency is part of the picture, it makes it so much harder for the addict or alcoholic to recover.

How come? Well, as I've mentioned in the previous section, when a big part of your relationship is all about evading criticism and evaluation, your relationship is fed by lies.

Your partner knows that every time you ingest heroin into your veins, you are rolling the dice and may end up dead. Any objective person can see that. But since you're in a codependent relationship, she or he cannot tell you that what you're doing is wrong.

Instead, she's afraid that she will lose you when she puts her foot down and says, "You have to either stop doing drugs, or I'm going to hit the door. I'm going to leave your life."

Codependent relationships are based on lies and not objective reality. And that's why drug addiction, or any other kind of substance addiction – or maybe even sex addiction, gossip addiction, Facebook addiction – or any kind of addictive behavior that leads to negative outcomes is almost impossible to resolve when codependency is part of the picture.

Addiction and Codependency Leads to Worse and Worse Situations

If you think the situation I've set up earlier seems depressing and discouraging enough, wait. It gets even worse.

When you are in a codependent relationship with somebody who has an addiction problem, this leads to more dishonesty, emotional manipulation, and low-level resentment.

You have to understand that the person who loves you knows that you are addicted to a substance. They, after all, have eyes. They can see the truth. But they are also addicted to your approval.

You may be addicted to chemical substances, but they are equally addicted to the relationship. So, this leads to an ever-spiraling mix of manipulation, dishonesty, and resentment.

It's not unusual for partners to say, "Well, if you really love me, you wouldn't judge me. You say that I'm an alcoholic. Okay, I like to drink. But I thought you loved me."

Do you see the emotional manipulation there? Well, nobody is being helped by that. Because that person that you're saying that to is being educated as far as what they can and cannot share, and the truths that they can and cannot believe in.

This leads to resentment. It's not unusual for people who are caught up in such relationships to have a love/hate relationship with the addict.

Don't for a second think that this is just about chemical substances. For example, there are a lot of mothers with serious personality disorders. They're not necessarily addicts, but their children have this love/hate relationship with them.

They're very controlling, manipulative, and they make their children feel like garbage, but their kids cannot let them go or call them out. So, they get caught in this codependent relationship and it's toxic for everybody. It's as if everybody gets sicker with each passing year.

If you are in a codependent relationship, please understand that you need help. This is not something that just happens to every relationship. Your relationship is sick.

I know that's probably not the word you wanted to hear. I know you're probably thinking that I'm judging you, but I'm calling a spade a spade.

In fact, the reason why you're reading this book is because, I suspect, you agree. You are in a sick relationship because a relationship based on lies is not a healthy relationship.

Thankfully, you are reading the right book.

I suggest you seek the help of a professional, but at the same time, there is a tremendous amount that you can do on your own to correct your relationship before it inflicts further damage on both you and the other person in the codependent relationship.

Chapter 3: Let's Begin at the Start: How Codependency Develops

It's very easy to think that a codependent relationship basically just comes preformed. Like, you hook up with an addict, and before you know it, it's a codependent relationship.

You really don't know what happened. It's as if you can't quite put your finger on it. The relationship that you have with that person seemed like it was codependent from Day One.

Well, you might want to step back and focus on what you can remember from the beginning of the relationship.

If you allow yourself a healthy amount of honesty, it would become clearly apparent to you that your codependent relationship didn't "just happen." There were signs from the beginning, and you allowed it to happen.

I know that this is painful to hear. Nobody likes to feel that they brought this on themselves, but that's not my main point. My point is, if you allowed this to happen, then you can choose to do something about it. It's all a choice.

It's not like your partner pointed a gun at your head and said, "Okay, I'm addicted to shopping and you're just going to be this passive victim in the background while I use up your credit cards." It doesn't work out that way.

The fact that you are in a negative and toxic codependent relationship means that you allowed it at some point to happen. And this is the most empowering thing in the world.

I know that sounds crazy, but hear me out. If you allowed this to happen, this means only one thing: you had a choice. And if you can choose for things to turn out this way, you can also choose to heal the situation and turn it around.

The key here is whether you're going to wake up to and reclaim your power of choice in your relationship or not.

Just because it's sick and you feel that it's toxic and you know the damage that it does to you and your partner, it doesn't mean that you have to choose to be stuck or remain stuck. You do have something to say and you can do something about it.

So where does codependency come from? Well, it depends on the relationship. But here are the most common patterns as revealed by the research.

We Learn from an Early Age

For a lot of codependent people, they learn codependency from their parents. In other words, these men and women weren't just thrown into a relationship with somebody who had a problem, and before they know it, they're codependent. Usually, it doesn't work out that way. In many cases, their tendency to get sucked into codependent arrangements begin with their parents.

Maybe they have an alcoholic father or a drug abusing mother, or maybe they have a mother who likes to nag and say to her husband that she's a loser, or maybe they're in a weird family situation where the father's family hates the mother's family and this has poisoned their relationship. Whatever the case may be, the way the parents "solve" the conflicts of the relationship has a big impact on how the children of that relationship define "acceptable patterns."

If you notice that your mom is completely dependent on your father and defines herself solely based on her relationship to your father and what your father has achieved, don't be surprised if you develop the same mindset. After all, you bring to the relationship what you have.

You can only give what you have. If you picked up codependency from your parents, that's what you bring to the table.

In a study published in Mental Health America, many codependents find themselves in toxic relationships because they have an alcoholic parent.

It turns out that when a parent is alcoholic, this can easily lead to physical, sexual or emotional abuse. Also, there's abuse of the other partner, often the mother, in front of the kids.

The mother teaches the kids codependency by her actions. Instead of leaving the man who routinely beats her up or curses her out, the female chooses to remain. And, worse yet, tries to placate and cater to the needs of the abusive partner.

It's as if no matter how much pain she is put through, the more she tries to make the other partner happy because she feels, deep down inside, she is nothing without her husband.

In this context, kids are programmed to feel like "the caretaker" of other people in their lives. When they come across somebody with a serious mental issue or emotional problems or addiction issues, this caretaker mindset kicks in.

Little do they know it, but they get caught up in a codependent relationship. This is because they "inherited" the pattern from their parents.

Similarly, if a parent is emotionally absent from the lives of their children, the kids end up looking for partners who share this trait. How come? Since they spent a lot of their youth trying to attract the attention of the parent that is emotionally absent, they become people pleasers.

They are hungry for emotional validation and attention. They are drawn not to people who give them that attention, but to people who cannot give them that attention for whatever reason. In other words, they're drawn to people that remind them of their emotionally absent parent.

In the United States, this usually takes the form of the emotionally absent father. These fathers provide for their families financially.

It's not unusual for middle class families to have all the trappings of a middle-class household. Two cars in the garage, the house is paid for, food on the table, and all the financial security a middle-class family needs. All thanks to the hard work of the father.

The problem is, the family pays a high price for that security because the father is almost always out of the house. And when he is in the house, he his emotionally absent because he's always worried about where his next paycheck is going to come from and how the bills are going to get paid.

A lot of adult kids hold this against their fathers because they cannot see the context. And worse yet, they look for the same patterns from other people.

Childhood Stress Can Create Adulthood Codependency

In a study released in March 2014 in the journal Psychiatria Hungarica, when many subjects were asked about their childhood, a certain pattern emerged. Subjects who are in codependent relationships have a higher chance of coming from backgrounds involving childhood neglect or abuse.

According to researchers, kids early on learn how to adopt to living with difficult parents by constantly repressing their own needs and catering to the demands of their parents. This pattern is then set in stone and this is what the kids look for when they become adults. In fact, this is how they define a healthy relationship.

For instance, if a baby's emotional needs were not adequately taken care of by that kid's parents, this person can grow up trying to please other people to make up for the love that was missing in his or her life early on.

Similarly, if a kid grows up in an overprotective family environment, this child could easily become dependent on others for their needs. They never quite fully learn how to stand on their own as far as intellectual and emotional growth are concerned. They look for people who would make decisions for them. Those are the kinds of relationships they tend to get into.

Similarly, kids who grow up with parents who are perfectionists end up becoming people pleasers. They live to please others and turn their backs on their own personal feelings and needs. They're trying to live up to an impossible standard and this makes them feel really lousy inside. As accomplished as they may get, and as successful as they could be, nothing is good enough because their parents have set up impossible perfectionist standards.

Finally, if a child grew up in a household where shame and guilt are used to motivate the child to action, the kid can grow up to view having their personal needs met as selfish, so they become selfless by default. Not because they want to be selfless, but because they feel that anything else is selfish, and selfishness is a bad thing across the board.

All of these patterns lead to people with no real self-confidence. They have a broken sense of personal identity, and have a tough time with issues like self-esteem and self-worth.

It is not unusual for these people to find themselves in toxic relationships with abusive partners. In fact, they're set up for such one-sided manipulative and codependent arrangements because of the early patterns they have witnessed.

Codependency Also Arises in People Who Did Not Grow Up in Dysfunctional Homes

I don't want you to get the impression that the only way somebody can end up in a codependent relationship is if they had a certain family background. The truth is, codependency can also be learned even if you had a very well-adjusted childhood.

If you had a parent that is not emotionally absent and who was there for you and you had confidence growing up, you can still end up in a relationship riddled with codependency.

This happens when you are in a relationship and the other partner suddenly gets depressed, experiences setbacks, or becomes sick physically. When this happens, one coping mechanism after another can lead to a codependent situation.

Similarly, if you are in a relationship where, for whatever reason, there is abuse, then the coping options can lead to a codependent arrangement.

Chapter 4: Why Do People Get Stuck in Codependent Relationships?

It would be easy to assume that since we're dealing with adults, with their own capacity to make choices, that people can easily choose to leave codependent relationships. The problem is, most people don't.

The most common example of this is the battered wife. The female partner knows that her husband beats her up every time he gets drunk.

Anybody looking at the situation from the outside in can readily conclude that this is a sick relationship. That she is not getting anything out of it and it would be best for her to leave. But as she gets one black eye after another, which may ultimately lead to her being murdered, she can't find it in herself to leave.

The same applies to child abuse and sexual abuse at the hands of a parent. This is due to a wide collection of coping mechanisms and mental states.

It's really important to understand these so you can recognize them in yourself.

The problem with psychological and personality problems is that it's very easy to say that the other person has a problem. It's very easy to say that this is something that just happens to other people. But if you're really completely honest with yourself, you have these traits as well. And I suspect that you're reading this book because you know this.

But just in case that it's still unclear to you, let me break it down.

Codependents are Very Indecisive

The main problem with codependency is that you spend most of your mental and emotional resources trying to please other people. It's as if you live for the satisfaction and happiness of others. The more you focus on others, the more you lose touch with yourself.

Well, that's a problem because you have your own feelings, thoughts, desires and needs. Just because you don't think about these, it doesn't make them go away. You will always have these needs.

And when you roll yourself off from your emotional need for healing, completion and respect, you lose touch with your personal dignity and you define yourself almost completely based on things you cannot control.

You cannot control an abusive girlfriend, wife, husband, or boyfriend. You can give them the world, and they can still choose to repay you by beating you up or cheating on you. Obviously, you can't control that person. You can, however, control yourself.

But if you are in a codependent relationship, you're so focused outward that you become indecisive because the decision point is not based on what it should be based on, which is your needs and what makes sense to you. Instead, it's based completely on the requirements and needs of people and situations you cannot control.

Codependent People are Gripped by Fear

The biggest fear people stuck in codependent relationships suffer from is one of abandonment.

You feel that your life is going to completely fall apart if you leave your boyfriend who is a drug addict. You feel that you are a worthless person if you say to your mom, who is abusive, to get the hell out of your life. You feel that by letting them down, that this will somehow lead to them getting worse, or you living an empty life.

This is all fear. Because they don't define you. You will survive them. In fact, your sustenance does not come from them.

But unfortunately, the sense of abandonment is so strong that regardless of how much abuse you suffer at their hands or how powerless you feel as you witness them abuse themselves, you simply cannot leave. And this is all based on fear. And fear is a worthless cornerstone for a relationship.

You know you're in a codependent and sick relationship when fear is the foundation of that relationship – the fear of loss, the fear of abandonment, the fear of hurt feelings.

Real healthy relationships are based on desire, happiness, joy. This is mutual. You make each other happy. Not fear.

Codependents Stick Around because They Hope They Can Change the Other Person

Another reason why people are stuck in codependent relationships is because they have this vague hope that somehow, by them catering to the whims of their partner, that they somehow will change that person.

I don't know about you, but when you buy somebody drugs, you're not helping that person break their drug addiction. When you buy people bottles of alcohol, you're not going them any favors because they will remain alcoholics.

This is an illusion. This mental mirage arises from the fact that people caught in codependent relationships think that love is enough to overcome.

Well, there are many different kinds of love. There is such a thing as "tough love." Believe it or not, sometimes, if you truly love somebody, the best thing you can do for them is to cut them out and let them go.

And unfortunately, if you're in a codependent relationship, this is the last thing you want to think about because you define yourself based on your connection to this person.

This has a variation called "the martyr complex." You're basically thinking that you're being an ideal Christian by taking all the abuse this person is heaping at you.

Well, guess what? You're not changing that person by simply taking and taking and taking their abuse. Instead, you are encouraging them to become worse people. What you're doing is not an act of love but aiding and abetting destructive behavior.

Guess what? Rapists, murderers, thieves, and other people who engage in destructive behavior oftentimes have people in their lives who enable them that ultimately culminated in those destructive behaviors.

Do you think those people who are acting out of "Christian obligation" or family love wanted people to get murdered or robbed? Of course, not. But they failed to realize that what they were doing was simply enabling even worst outcomes to materialize.

Common Characteristics of Codependent People

What follows is a quick rundown of the common characteristics of people in codependent relationships.

If you see several of these traits in yourself, it's time to seek help. At the very least, take full advantage of the information I'm going to share with you in this book so you can be well on your way to recovery.

Please understand that the list below can only help you if you are completely honest with yourself.

This is no time for denial. This is no time to take refuge in the common excuses and justifications you give yourself because if you do that, you no longer think you have a problem. You start thinking that this is somebody else's problem.

Well, here's the thing. It's hard to quit being an alcoholic when you think you're not an alcoholic. A little bit of honesty goes a long way.

So, keep an open mind regarding the following characteristics of codependent people.

- You are extremely dependent on another person in your life. You think that without that person, you are nothing.

- You always feel responsible for somebody else's actions or feelings.

- You think that if you do something wrong, it's going to reflect badly on your family or this one person so you hold your tongue and you really watch what you do because everything comes back to that person and you don't want that person to be hurt.

- You're constantly trying to please others.

- You believe that one other person is so precious to you that it's okay for that person to abuse you, dominate you, or shame you.

- You find yourself neglecting your appearance, your physical shape, or your finances because the other person needs more help.

- You don't really know what you're feeling or what you think is good for you. You've lost sight of your goals that have nothing to do with that special person in your life.

- You think that your identity depends on your family or your relationship with that other person. You don't really think you are worthy of respect standing on your own. You're nothing special. You haven't really achieved anything or have much accomplishments in life except for your relationship with that person.

- You're excited to be with that other person in your life because she is just so unpredictable. And when she does something that she hasn't done before, you let her get away with it because she sets the boundaries in your relationship.

- You have a tough time admitting that your relationship is far from perfect or even normal.

- You spend a lot of time trying to change people's minds regarding that special person in your life or you try to spend a lot of money or effort trying to change your physical environment so as to make that other person more comfortable or give that person what they want.

- As much as you love that special person in your life, part of you wants to leave that person. Part of you doesn't like how that person treats you. You label your relationship as bittersweet.

- You're scared to death of being left alone, ignored, or not given the "attention" you feel you deserve from that other person. The idea of that person not being in your life makes you sick.

- You find yourself comparing yourself or your relationship to other people or other people's relationships. You always look at your partner as better than either you or other people. You feel that you are better than other people because you have that special person in your life.

- You rarely talk about yourself. You find that when you brag, you're really bragging about the fact that that other person is in your life and is somehow connected to you.

- You come from a family of abuse, addiction, or mental and emotional dysfunction.

- You experience symptoms of depression

Please note that depression does not equal sadness. Melancholy is just part of depression. It's not always present.

You can feel depressed when you feel that life is meaningless or it lacks substance. It's not quite fulfilling. What makes the depression is that it lingers from day to day.

People in codependent relationships experience depression in contexts of their relationship. When they're trying to please the other partner, they feel that the relationship is missing something. It's lacking a special ingredient and they always feel off-centered, restless, incomplete. This is depression.

- Anxiety

You experience all sorts of unrealistic fears regarding your partner leaving you or feeling hurt. You feel really protective on a 24/7 basis that somehow, some way, somebody might hurt her or say something bad to her and you feel bad that you can't be there for that special person in your life.

This crosses over to clinical anxiety precisely because this happens on a continuous basis. It's chronic. It's not just something that you worry because you observed facts or something actually happened that would reasonably trigger this. Instead, this is just a generalized fear.

- Stress

Codependent people feel a tremendous amount of stress because they always feel that they are tired mentally.

They keep thinking about their relationship and the other person in the relationship. They think about the fact that they have certain unmet needs in their relationship, but somehow, if they stick with it and they try to change the other person, things will work out.

This gives a tremendous amount of stress because of the fact that you're basically grinding your gears on a 24/7 basis. This happens on both a conscious and subconscious level.

Sometimes it fluctuates in intensity, but when your mind is always caught up with issues regarding your relationship, it poisons your mindset.

This tremendous amount of stress wears you down. You don't give yourself permission to fully rest.

You know you're in a normal relationship when you trust your partner because trust brings rest.

You don't have to worry about her screwing another guy. You don't have to worry about your father abandoning your family. You don't have to worry about your mother degrading her children or abusing them. Instead, you trust them, and this gives you rest.

You don't have to stress because you know, if you trust somebody and you have good reason to trust them, you can turn your focus on something else or just chill.

You don't have this in a codependent relationship. You feel that since you're responsible for the fitness and the happiness of the relationship, that you have to commit to the constant output of this emotional energy.

- Low Emotional Expression

Ironically, people in codependent relationships look numb. When you look at them in terms of their emotional expressiveness, they look like they've been through a lot of stress and/or traumatic experiences so they can only have a narrow range of emotional expression.

That's the irony of codependency. Because of the tremendous stress that's been taking out in them, they're basically emotionally tired all the time.

But don't let that fool you. Deep down inside you're struggling with depression, anxiety, numbness, and a vague sense that your own personal identity is slipping away.

- You're constantly thinking about your mistakes

You know you're in a codependent relationship when you spend a ridiculous amount of your time thinking about how you screwed up and whether your partner would notice.

It can be a very small thing. Maybe you didn't take the dry cleaning to her place on time. Most women would forgive that readily. In fact, they wouldn't even notice it.

But you make a big deal out of it because somehow, some way, you think that it speaks volumes about how much you care about her and that if she finds out, this might be the end of your relationship.

So, what do you do? You try to overcome and overcompensate by fixating on this mistake. At the very least, you're just mentally grinding and emotionally playing out that scenario over and over.

- You feel the desire to be liked by everyone

This is especially true of people who are respected and cared for by your significant other. This person is so important to you that you have put it on yourself to be liked by everybody that she likes.

Accordingly, you spend a tremendous amount of time trying to be somebody you're not. You try hard to be all people to everyone you meet.

I'm sure you already know the futility of all of this because you can't please everybody all the time. That's just not going to happen. You're going to drive yourself crazy and you're just going to make yourself sick.

- You confuse love with pity

It's very easy for you to play the victim in your relationship because you think that the more your significant other tries to care for you because you got hurt or you got shortchanged, that this is real love. No, it's not.

There's a big difference between love and pity. Love requires respect. Pity doesn't.

Pity is compassion. You can have pity on a cat that got run over by a car by the side of the road, but that isn't love.

And unfortunately, people in a codependent relationship would take whatever they can get. And that's why the more pitiful they feel and the bigger the victim they imagine themselves to be, the more they think they're worthy of love.

This leads to a sick arrangement where the partner can physically abuse them and the codependent would hang on for dear life. Or, worse yet, feed the addiction.

This plays out when the partner is a sex addict. So, basically, she's bringing other men home, or he's bringing other women home, and you're there to enable him or her. That's how bad confusing love and pity can be.

The relationship is no longer about both of you, but about the other partner exclusively. It's about her needs, her fulfillment, her realization as a full human being. Forget about you. You're just there as a supporting cast.

Is that the kind of relationship you want for yourself? Is that how you define maturity, responsibility and happiness? It's sick. It's twisted. And ultimately, it's unsustainable.

In Chapter 5, I'm going to give you an overview of the self-help techniques you can use to overcome codependency.

Chapter 5: Overcoming Codependency: 6 Techniques

In this chapter, I'm going to give you an overview of the six techniques. I will teach you so you can overcome codependency. You already know how toxic a codependent relationship can be. You already know the damage it can do, not just to yourself but to those people around you who love you.

In this chapter, I'm going to give you a quick overview, and in the succeeding chapters, we will drill down on each of these self-help techniques. Please understand that you should not look at any information in this book as some sort of license to forego the services of mental and emotional care professionals.

If you look into this book as a starting point, and if you need professional help, by all means, get it. This book is intended, at best, to be supplemental to any other kind of formal help that you could get.

Admit that you are codependent

The first step in overcoming codependency is to admit reality. Just like with any other problem or issue, if you don't admit that you have a problem, it's going to be impossible to change. If an alcoholic doesn't think she has a problem, then she is not going to put down the bottle; it's that simple. So admission is a necessary first step.

Assert your personal boundaries

All of us, as mature, responsible adults, have the right to set our own personal boundaries. These involve what we can and will not do. These involve who we are, and who don't want to be. All of us, as living, breathing, mature adults, have this capacity.

Just because you've been in a relationship for so long, where you feel you've lost this capacity, doesn't mean that you have actually lost it. You can choose to take ownership of this capacity. Because when you do this, your relationships become more fulfilling.

Your partner no longer treats you like some sort of emotional doormat. They can no longer treat you for granted because you have certain lines that you would not cross.

Prioritize self-care

A lot of people in codependent relationships think that the moment they start taking care of themselves, and prioritizing their needs, that they're somehow selfish. They've gotten this idea in their heads that if they are selfish, then this means that they are evil, they're bad, there's something wrong with them; that's garbage.

Let's put it this way: If you want to take care of somebody else, you have to first take care of yourself. Because if you don't take care of yourself, you won't be able to care for them as well. It really is that basic. When you get your head right, then you will be able to truly help those around you.

But if you continue to be sick and allow your head and emotions to be filled with toxic ideas and mindsets, then whatever "help" you try to give others will ultimately fall flat. Your efforts will always be contaminated by feelings of fear of rejection, guilt, and an abiding sense of emptiness; not exactly healthy.

Discover and practice self-compassion

Let's get one thing clear: Nobody can love you more than yourself, not another person, not here, not now, not ever. You have to love yourself. This is non-negotiable. Because if you feel that somebody else will complete you, you will always remain dependent on that person.

And if you're completely honest about it, this will fill you with resentment, because they have to take care of themselves first. So if you feel that only that person can love, and that person loves herself first, what happens to the relationship as far as you're concerned?

So do yourself a big favor and practice self-compassion. Love yourself first, see your value and worth as a human being. Understand that you deserve respect and dignity. Nobody can give these to you unless you give them to yourself first.

This is crucial because if you do not stand up for yourself in your relationships, then who knows where you'll stand up for these. Your career may be lackluster and unfulfilling. Your health may suffer because you don't invest enough time for yourself.

There are so many areas in your life where lack of self-compassion can lead to hurt, pain, failure, frustration, and unhappiness. The good news is you can choose to practice self-compassion. This is a choice, nobody can give this to you.

Build a strong support system around you

Please understand that while you think you are responsible for other people, that it all doesn't have to rest on your shoulder. When you feel the stress and pressure of always having to give, give, and give, you don't do yourself any favors when you think that it has to necessarily involve you alone.

When you build a strong support system where your allies, friends, and family members supporting you, you find the strength that you need to get out from under the codependent patterns you find yourself in.

Just as it doesn't make sense to try to carry the relationship alone, you shouldn't try to bear the whole weight of overcoming code-dependency alone.

Always be ready to seek professional help

If you think about it, unlike mental illnesses like depression and anxiety, schizophrenia, obsessive-compulsive disorder, and others, code-dependency, generally speaking, doesn't involve biochemical transmitters in the brain.

In other words, this is usually a disorder of how you adapt to your circumstances and the relationships you find yourself in. This is what makes it difficult because when you're clinically depressed, there are lots of pharmaceutical products out there that can shift the balance of your brain chemistry so you feel less depressed. The same goes with anxiety and other mental and emotional conditions.

Code-dependency, on the other hand, involves a series of choices and mindsets. And that's why they're so hard to treat and overcome on your own. When you work with a professional, they can monitor and track your situation, so they can give you feedback that enables you to start looking at certain common signals in a different way, which can lead you to take actions that can produce different outcomes. At the very least, you will learn how to rediscover yourself and identify self-destructive patterns.

Chapter 6: Admit That You Are a Codependent

Make no mistake, admitting that you are codependent is one of the hardest things to do, because hey, let's face it, nobody likes to think that there's something wrong with them. How do you feel when somebody says you're wrong? Or there's something wrong with you, or what you're doing is not right?

Of course, you feel defensive. Your number-one instinct is to deny that there is something wrong. And guess what, we do this to ourselves. But as I have mentioned in the overview chapter, until and unless you admit that you are a code-dependent, you're not going to get any better.

Forget it, kiss that idea good-bye. It's just not going to happen. How come? Well, it all boils down to how open your mind is to a solution. You have to understand that for you to look for a solution, you must first believe that there is a problem.

If you don't think that what you're doing, and how you're thinking, and how you're relating to others around you, as well as the life you're living is code-dependent, then there's no need for a solution, because there's no problem. Do you see how this works?

You're reading this book for a reason. You're not happy, you feel that your life is drifting and not going to where you want it to go. You are not living the kind of life you would like for yourself. It's okay to admit that. It's okay to say that you are codependent. Once you are able to say it, believe it.

In a study released in February 2000, in the psychological journal, Genetic, Social And General Psychology Monographs, researchers found that code-dependency can be traced to family background. This is not an absolute determinant, but when we see patterns in our family history, this can lead us to codependent patterns.

In other words, when you come from a family that has historic stressors like mental illness, alcoholism, drug abuse, sexual abuse, physical abuse, or a physically ill parent like Alzheimer's, or polio, or some other debilitating disease, these stresses accumulate in terms of life lessons that can lead to codependent behaviors.

Being aware that you had such a background is crucial to healing. But to think that you had a perfect childhood, or a perfect background where there is absolutely no chance of any kind of stressor leading to the kind of dysfunctional relationships you have is not going to help anybody.

So a little bit of awareness regarding your family background, past experiences, and past trauma can open your mind to the possibility that you are a code-dependent.

A little bit of denial can crush the healing process

If you want to overcome code-dependency, you have to be completely honest; this is crucial. You have to say that your father had a problem, or your mother had issues, or you did not do what you needed to do, that there's something with your decisions.

The problem with this, according to the same research study I cited above, families that are dysfunctional usually do not acknowledge that they are suffering problems. It's as if there's an 800-pound elephant in the room, and mom and dad deny that daddy has a gambling problem, or mom is sex-addict, or your uncle is addicted to certain types of food, and some people are alcoholics in the family.

It has all these dysfunctions, and everybody can see it, but the way they live their lives. It's as if it's invisible; again, like an elephant in the room. Everybody's uncomfortable, they're dancing around these issues, but ultimately, the whole family dynamic is driven by one factor: The avoidance of shame.

People deny that they have problems because they don't want to feel ashamed. They think that admitting that they have certain issues is a sign of weakness, that it's some sort of defect. If we are completely honest with ourselves, all of us have problems. It may not be the same problems, but they're problems nonetheless.

Some people are addicted to drugs, others are addicted to Facebook and gossip. And you may be thinking, "Well, Facebook and gossip, those are much tolerable addictions than drugs or alcohol. Well, think again.

If you are gripped by so much fear as to what to post on your Facebook wall, and what kind of post to like or not like, then it's only a matter of time until you realize that you're not free. You're not being honest with yourself.

You're suppressing a key part of your personality, and ultimately, you are dependent on other people's approval. You're trying to be something that you're not. You're a fraud, a liar. And the worst part to all of this is that it starts so innocently, until it starts to poison other areas of your life, and then before you know it, you're living a giant lie.

Welcome to the club, because if you are dealing with any kind of personal weakness issue or addiction, it involves these issues. The severity may be different, but we're talking about differences in degree, not in kind.

So dispense with this black-and-white division in your mind of thinking, "Well, at least that's not my problem, or at least my issue is not that bad." Well, you can play that game with yourself all you want, but it's not going to help you overcome your issues until, and unless you see it for the problem that it is.

Dysfunctional families continue to become dysfunctional because they play these games, and they stop seeing serious problems because they're always making excuses. They're always engaged in euphemisms, and essentially, just trying to cover up everything by not talking about them or confronting them.

Make no mistake, family confrontations are not pleasant. After all, these are people you love, these are people who are closest to you. I'm sure you already know that the people that can hurt you the most are the ones closest to you emotionally.

So it's not surprising that a lot of people would really walk on eggshells as far as their loved ones are concerns. But the problem is the more you deny, the more those problems will grow. If your father beats the hell out of your mom, he is not being helped when you choose to be blind about that situation.

Similarly, if your mother is addicted to sleeping pills, nobody's being helped when you choose to make all sorts of excuses, or justifications for that kind of behavior. You have to first accept that there's something wrong. You have to call it by its proper name.

This is why you have to overcome the dysfunctional coping mechanisms that you may have learned from your family. It all starts with family programming. Acknowledge that you are a code-dependent; this is the first step to recovery.

Step #1
Be completely honest with yourself, describe what is happening. Strip away any kind of justification, excuse or any kind of word game you normally play with yourself. Call your situation for what it is.

Step #2
Realize that you have your own needs. Understand that it's perfectly okay to have your own needs. You deserve to be respected, you deserve to be loved. You deserve to be accepted on your own. Not because you are part of a family, not because you're in a relationship.

Not because you're in a relationship, not because you were a good person and you did certain things, and you have certain achievements. No, just based on who you are, right here, right now, you deserve love, acceptance and respect. Accept this, acknowledge this. Realize that this is real.

Step #3
Look to other people to understand what you're feeling. Please understand that just because you're asking for help, or you open yourself up to help, that it doesn't mean you're weak. It doesn't mean you're crazy. It doesn't mean there's something wrong with you.

Instead, it just means that you're human, and this is perfectly healthy. Knowing and admitting that you need help, whether professional or otherwise, are signs that you are a strong person. This doesn't mean that there's something wrong with you. This doesn't mean that you're weak. This doesn't mean that you are beyond help. This definitely doesn't mean you're immoral. Instead, it's perfectly okay to seek help for your problem.

Step #4
Forget about rejection

One of the main reasons why people, who have serious problems with code-dependency, fail to get the help that they desperately need because they're afraid of rejection. Rejection takes many different forms.

You're hurting deep down inside, and when you ask somebody to help you, they laugh at you, or they pretend that they didn't hear anything. Deep down inside you know what happened, but on a surface level, you make up all sorts of excuses and explanations to cover up for the sense of rejection and abandonment you feel.

Please understand that when it comes to mental and emotional recovery, the fear of rejection is worse than actual rejection. Seriously, when you fear rejection you're basically walking on egg shells, and making up all sorts of stories, and coming up with all sorts of schemes not to get help.

In other words, year after year, you continue to get worse in your codependent relationship because you take refuge in all these elaborate lies you set up for yourself. These lies are built on the fear of rejection.

Let me tell you, if you were to ask for help from ten people that you know, all ten of them will not reject you. I'm sure some of them will, but those are the odds we are dealt with. But not all of them will reject you, so get the idea of rejection out of your head. Focus instead on your need for recovery.

Step #5
Commit to recovering from code-dependency

One common game many abused women play on themselves is the idea that code-dependency is not that serious, that this is just a simple personality issue; maybe they're just being sensitive. So they try to sweep it under the rug, and sadly, some of them end up dead.

They're in a codependent relationship, and before you know it, the other partner becomes so abusive, the situation becomes so unbearable, and they end up six feet underground. I don't mean to scare you, but this is the kind of risk you run when you are in a codependent relationship.

You have to stop playing this game with yourself. You have to get the support that you need from others, and it's perfectly okay. This is not a source of shame, because all of us need help at some level or other. Just some of us are more mature than others, and that's why we admit that we need help.

So you have to admit this. You have to be big enough to do this, because until and unless you open yourself up for help in code-dependency recover, nothing's going to change. In fact, things will probably get worse.

If you think your mother is oppressive and nasty now, wait until you see what she's up to five years from now. If you think your kids are mean to you now, wait until what happens when it is time for you to retire. It's not going to get better.

Focus on opening yourself up to getting the help you need, so you can slay the code-dependency dragon right here, right now. It all boils down to setting boundaries, and loving yourself first so you can then end up loving those around you better, and in a healthier way.

Chapter 7: Assert Your Personal Boundaries

You have to understand that the reason why people suffer in silence in codependent relationships, is because they have lost sight of any kind of sensible boundary. It's as if they live solely for the relationship. They're only their father's son, or they're only their mother's daughter, or their husbands' possession or their wives' chauffeur or driver.

These issues bubble to the surface precisely because people have lost sight of personal boundaries and definitions. They no longer believe in them. It's as if they don't exist. Before they know it, they no longer have a sense of self. Instead, they view themselves as simply part of something larger, involving, of course, the outsize personality or needs of the other partner.

They're part of a family. They're part of a team. They're part of a mission. They're part of a goal. Well, let's cut the crap. These are just excuses you give yourself for not standing up for your rights and standing up for your own personality.

You can be your own person, and still be part of something larger. Winners do this, happy people do this, but your situation is sick and unhappy precisely because you think that it's either or. In other words, for the team to win, your identity has to be completely subsumed or incorporated into the team.

So it's no longer your voluntary contribution of talents, efforts and energy to a shared goal that's going on. Instead, you feel that you have to give everything to that other person and lose yourself for you to matter.

And the worst part to all of this is you rob yourself the ability to even talk about it. And before you know it, you can't even talk about it because you've forgotten it. You have thought of yourself as part of something bigger for so long that you have forgotten the most basic steps of communication.

It is no surprise that given that given this background, that codependent people experience emotional abuse. They just get stepped on all the time. In fact, it reaches the point where the dominant partner in the relationship automatically assumes you'd bend over, that if they take your money, they take your time, emotional labor, they don't even ask, because it's already a given.

And sadly, you're not doing yourself any favors because they only need to look at what happened thousands of times before. Remember, people are not stupid, people do look at patterns. If somebody sees that you keep doing something over and over again thousands of times before, what do you think they will think?

In fact, they may be thinking to themselves that they're just being efficient. Why should they go through the motions of asking for your consent when you have demonstrated thousands of times over that you will give your consent; you will go along to get along. So what's the point of even asking you for permission?

When they reach this stage, the psychological abuse becomes intense, because you then get caught up in a love-hate relationship. You live for that other person but you're crying out deep down inside for some semblance of acknowledgment.

But the problem is you have enabled that person to keep taking, and taking, and taking by just giving without question. You only have yourself to blame precisely because you have let go of your boundaries. You feel that you cannot live without them. You have subsumed your identity to theirs. They're in control. They define the relationship.

Please understand that this is happening in your head. They may not be thinking about this. They may not find your relationship in these terms, but the problem is you are their teacher. If you say to your partner in so many words, and as revealed by your actions, that it's perfectly okay to step on you, and treat you like some sort of emotional doormat, what do you think they'll do?

They will do that. That is the human condition. When given an inch, most people will take a mile. That's just the way it is. That's the nature of the beast. This is why you have to stand up for your boundaries. Clearly delineate what you can and cannot do. Clearly describe what are off-limits to you. Demand limitations in your relationship.

The first part to all of this is to be clear about the fact that you are not the other person in the relationship. In other words, you first create internal boundaries. When you start defining yourself as your boyfriend, your girlfriend, your spouse, or as part of a family or team, there is no internal boundary because their victory is yours, their struggle is yours.

And this might sound awesome on the surface, but this is very troubling indeed, because there are no boundaries. There is no demarcation line for responsibility. So the first step is to draw a line between what you're responsible for and what you attribute to the other person.

This means that you have to have your own thoughts, your own feelings, your own needs. These are yours, can you remember them? Can you talk about them? Can you describe them? Mentally and emotionally healthy people take responsibility for their own emotions.

In other words, you say to yourself, "I'm okay when I feel this way. I'm okay that I have these feelings." And then the next step of being emotionally and mentally healthy, is you take responsibility for the actions you take because of your emotions.

Codependent people cannot do this. Instead, they feel that they're just driven to do certain things because they're part of the team that they're doing this for love, that they're just driven by passion. What they're doing is that they are acting blindly.

You have to remember that the world doesn't care about your emotions and your intentions. It couldn't care less. However, the world does sit up and pay attention once you take action on those emotions.

Your actions change your world. You actions trigger your destiny. That's how you change your reality. And the problem is codependent people have completely lost sight of this, because they think that whatever they are feeling is just part of what they've become in the relationship. They have lost sight of the fact that they can actually choose what to think, which can lead to choices on how to feel and how to act.

They are no longer acting like mental and emotional adults. Instead, a codependent is essentially a child; and the worst form of child. They take the responsibility for the problems of others. They take it on themselves, because they are carrying everything for the team.

Try as they might to walk out of th relationship, they feel they can't because they've lost the courage to even choose to do so. Sounds sad, right? Sounds pathetic. I'm sure this also sounds familiar.

In a University of North Dakota 1990 study, codependent women and men, who were studied, these people remained loyal to their romantic partners despite the tremendous amount of emotional stress they're subjected to with a matching lack of reward.

In other words, they're in a relationship where the partner just sucks in emotional support and gives nothing back. This study involved 19 men and 31 women. They went through a code-dependency counseling system, and took a test to determine their level of code-dependency.

The test that they took was the Friel's Code-Dependency Assessment Inventory. They were asked to fill out background information. This information is then cross-referenced with 30 random people taken from the general population.

This cross-comparison group was viewed by the researchers as a control group.

The study revealed that women and men showed different dependency characteristics. Codependent women tend to be codependent when it comes to the expectation of change, the expectation of being rescued, self-worth, the exaggerated responsibility they feel for the happiness of others, and a distorted sense of control over their relationships.

According to the study, codependent men focused more an exaggerated sense of responsibility for the welfare of their partner and a distorted sense of control. The study highlights the fact that regardless of whether you are a codependent man or woman, your warped view regarding these issues means that you have lost your sense of boundaries and limits in your relationship.

Women, in particular, are susceptible to thinking that they are responsible for other people's happiness. Similarly, in a 2012 study published in the journal of consumer research, 120 students were studied in terms of their ability to resist temptation.

This study highlights the power of phrasing or mindset when it comes to willpower and control. This has a strong impact on codependent relationships, because ultimately, the way you define your role in your relationship has a strong predictive role in the outcomes and happiness level of that relationship.

In the study, 120 students were split into 2 groups. They were tempted with ice cream. One group was told that they should say to themselves, "I can't eat ice cream." The other group, on the other hand, were told to say, "I don't eat ice cream."

Once the students were tempted with the ice cream, they are then asked to answer a number of questions, that on their face, were not really related to the study. Once they finished answering the questions, they handed in their answers, and the test-taker offered them a free treat.

They were asked to choose between a chocolate candy bar and a healthier snack. The researcher would note what kind of snack the students chose. Interestingly enough, when respondents said that they can't eat ice cream, they are more likely to select the chocolate candy bar.

This happened 61% of the time. Of the students who were told to say that they don't eat ice cream, only 36% selected the chocolate candy bar. This study shows that the way we describe our mindset and our capabilities plays a big role in how we handle difficult choices.

In other words, how you define yourself in your relationship has a strong impact on whether you would be able to overcome code-dependency, or whether these negative patterns will persist. It may seem like a small difference because we're talking about just words, but there is a big difference when it comes to actions between saying "I can't" and "I don't."

When you say I can't, you're basically talking about your ability to choose. Maybe your circumstances prevent you from doing so that's why you can't do certain things. But "I can't" essentially means a changeable physical state.

You're basically saying, "I can't do it right now because of these other things going on. If they change, I may be able to do something different." Accordingly, you're more likely to be dependent on your circumstances as you define them.

Saying "I don't" on the other hand, is an expression of character. "This is who I am. I don't eat meat. I don't drink. I don't do drugs. I don't do that kind of stuff." This is an expression of identity. And it may seem that a lot of Americans would use these words interchangeably.

But psychologically speaking, they have a world of difference between them. If you want to be motivated in breaking free of codependent patterns in your relationships, you have to look at the power of choice you have. And this is rooted in the identity you choose.

When you say "I don't," you are reflecting the fact that you have the power to choose. "I don't do that. That's not just who I am. I can choose to do that, but I don't." Compare this with "I can't." You feel that your hands are tied, and the circumstances are working against you. Psychologically, it's a more limiting feeling.

So if you want to break free of certain negative behaviors in you codependent relationship, start using the phrase "I don't" more often. According to research, saying "I can't" drains you psychologically and saps you of your will power. Focus instead of "I don't."

Step-By-Step Guide To Setting Your Personal Boundaries

Step #1
Be honest and know yourself

Without considering your partner in the relationship, ask yourself what you can live with and what your non-negotiable's are. Again, assume that that person is not in your life. If you are under emotional pressure from your parents, assume that they're dead.

Ask yourself, what can you live with and what are the things that are non-negotiable with you. You have to have the confidence to demand these things. These are your boundaries. These are what you will expect other people to respect. They can't cross into them. When you demand these, you expect other people to stop. These are the things that you say you don't do.

Step #2
Cross-reference the boundaries you think you have by asking other people

Communicate the boundaries you've chosen by having honest conversations with other people. Your boundaries are not going to set themselves. They're not going to implement themselves automatically. You have to be able to communicate them to the person that you want to respect them.

This is not going to be easy because you have obviously, habitually let them step over your boundaries. For example, you and your partner have a child, and you want your partner to take care of the child more. You have to be clear about what this means.

Be as specific as possible. Does this mean read to your child? Does this mean give them a bath? Does this mean take them to school? Be as specific as possible. This is key to an effective and honest conversation.

Compare this with saying to your partner, "You're not around to take care of your baby." How do you think that will make them feel? How effective do you think that is? Instead, they feel judged. They feel that you're trying to trap them, and this doesn't help your relationship as well as your efforts at breaking free from code-dependency.

Be as specific as possible and explain the impact those actions may have. To your partner, it may seem like you just want him or her to take the child to the park. But when you explain what this means to you and to the child, they start to get it, and they start to see what your boundaries are, and what, they start to respect you more, because ultimately, they start seeing your shared goals and your shared objectives.

But when you phrase this in terms of what they are doing wrong, or how unfair your situation, or how uneven your relationship is, it becomes a contest. They start to pull back, and they start to manipulate you, and you start to say things that you would regret later on, and nobody is being helped.

Step #3
Say No more often

Please understand that you always have the right to say no. You don't have to do it. Just because it has happened many times before, doesn't necessarily mean that it has to continue to happen forever until you're dead. You can say No.

But it's important to explain why. The explanation must not be like trying to please the other person, or trying to somehow butter the other person. No, you have to say why you're saying No as far as your own physical, mental and emotional health are concerned.

Why are you saying No, and why isn't doing otherwise the best for you? Because if you are able to separate these two issues, then you would know that this is not about you being selfish, or egotistic. This doesn't mean that you no longer care about other people, or you're lacking compassion.

Instead, you're making it clear that by saving a little bit for yourself, you ensure that there's a lot more of you to share with your loved ones. This is part of self-care and self-love.

Step #4
Consciously stop trying to be a people-pleaser

I can talk on and on about establishing personal boundaries, but until and unless you step up to the conclusion that you can't live your life trying to please other people all the time, you're not going to achieve much progress.

How do you know you're not being a people-pleaser? The better way to answer this is by asking the opposite question: How do you know you're being a people-pleaser? It's actually quite simple: When you are doing something that you normally don't want to do, and you find yourself doing it quite a bit, you're being a people-pleaser.

If you find yourself noticing that you're being emotionally manipulated to do something that you normally would not want to do, you're being a people-pleaser. Here's the secret: Understand that you cannot control other people's needs. You can't control what they choose to do with their lives.

You can only control one person in this world, you can control yourself. So do yourself a big favor and pay close attention to how you normally react or respond to other people's requirement for help. Please understand that it's perfectly okay to say No if they are constantly asking you to do something that you don't like to do.

It's okay to do it once in a while, but if they have gotten into the habit of constantly asking you to do it, that's going to be a problem. This is especially true if they dispense with asking you altogether. It's as if they assume that you will do it. They've taken you for granted, they're no longer respecting you.

Retake your dignity by first asking to be asked, and most importantly, say No from time to time, and then eventually, just refusing to do the things that you normally don't want to do.

Step #5
Be ready to impose consequences

Let me tell you, if you say No all the time, but people still step on you anyway and you don't do anything about it, your No is worthless. I wanted to get that out of the way. You can't look at this chapter as a simple case of you going through the motions.

What's the point of showing an appearance of autonomy when you don't have real autonomy? Real autonomy can only happen when there are consequences. So when people make a request, and you say No, and they continue to press, you have to step in and say there will be consequences. Meaning, "I'm not going to do it."

That's how they know you're serious. That's how they know you mean it. The worst thing that can happen is when you allow yourself to feel guilty that you said no to others. Because eventually, the boundaries are going to get obscure again.

For your boundaries to be real, they have to be observed. Focus on what you stand to gain, because the more you say No, the higher the chance that your code-dependency will end and your marriage will survive.

This can mean the difference between loneliness, abandonment and pain. It's not easy because you're used to doing things a certain way for so long, but the more you stand on your rights, and the more you establish these boundaries, the more better things become for your relationship, and eventually, it's the best thing that can happen to your partner. They would start behaving like responsible and mature adults.

Chapter 8: Prioritize Self Care

You may imagine yourself as the center of your family. You may think that you must be strong and provide for the rest of your family, otherwise, everybody will just fall apart.

A lot of codependent people think that they are always at the center of whatever relationship they're in. After all, they give, give and give some more.

You have to start with this assumption. We all know that this is an unhealthy assumption and, sooner or later, you would have to turn your back on this kind of thinking.

But even if we were to go with this assumption, please understand that continuing with the current codependent structure of your relationship will actually harm the people you think you care about.

In other words, by taking care of yourself better, you would be able to provide better care to those around you.

Ironically, the more you step away from the codependent arrangements and duties and responsibilities you have assumed for yourself, the more likely you will be able to provide the right kind of support and welfare to those around you. That's one way of looking at self-care.

By taking better care of yourself, you become a better care provider. Whether that care takes the form of physical, emotional, spiritual or psychological care, it doesn't matter. By taking care of number one first, you ensure that there's a lot more leftover to share with other people.

On the other hand, you should look at self-care as crucial to your wellbeing as an independent person. Please understand that nobody's going to love you better than yourself.

A lot of people would say that you complete them, that they have what you're missing, but these are lies. You have to already come in complete to the relationship. Otherwise, it's not much of a relationship at all.

It's a codependent relationship. Meaning, it's sick. And it leads to abuse, pain and loss. So, regardless of how you look at it, self-care is crucial and it has to be top priority.

Science backs this up. In a Brazilian study released in January 2016, 505 families participated in a codependency study where at least one family member was abusing drugs. Their call patterns to a drug prevention hotline were logged, and the data derived from the study proved to be useful when it comes to measuring codependency because the participants were asked to complete assessments involving their level of codependency.

Of the 505 family members interviewed during the study, 64% indicated a high level of codependency as measured by the Holyoke Codependency Index (HCI). Interestingly enough, the vast majority of codependent interviewees were either the wives and mothers of these drug users.

Naturally, flowing from this codependent relationship, family members of drug abusers suffered a tremendous amount of stress. And we're not just talking about mental and emotional stress, but also physical manifestations of stress.

In fact, these family codependent structures were so strong that the children in those families actually have a higher chance of becoming drug addicts themselves. This then leads to a general decline in both the physical and psychological health of these families compared to the general population.

I start this chapter on self-care with this startling study's findings to highlight the point that if you want to properly take care of your family, the best thing you can do is to take care of yourself first.

You have to understand that the respondents of these codependency studies involving drug abusers were female care providers for their families.

Obviously, they wanted the best for their families. They really cared about family members.

But the problem is, when they're caught up in codependent relationships, they are unable to provide the wellbeing their family needs.

In other words, since they weren't taking care of themselves enough to break out of this codependent arrangement, they end up doing a lousy job and everybody else suffers. The end result of this, of course, are kids in these families becoming drug users themselves.

In a 2006 study in the *British Journal of Health Psychology*, researchers identified physical exercise as one basic way to practice self-care.

You may be thinking, after looking at the Brazilian study results, that self-care has to somehow involve something out of the ordinary. You might be thinking that you have to be some sort of hero or go through some sort of 12-step program or specialized training. While it can definitely do that, you can start with something simpler.

Believe it or not, just by exercising on a regular basis, you can improve not only your physical health, but your emotional health as well.

This *British Journal of Health Psychology* study showed that when people adopt a regular exercise program, they not only develop better physical health, but their emotional and mental health improves as well.

According to the surveys of the test participants, people responded favorable improvements across the board. What are we talking about? Well, people improved their study habits, of all things. They were able to stick to their commitments.

They're more likely to do their fair share of household chores. They also are more likely to exhibit stronger control over their emotions. They are more likely to eat healthy, drink less caffeine and alcohol, and stop smoking.

In terms of emotional issues, they report less emotional distress and, interestingly enough, less physical stress. And all it took was just regular exercise.

Keep in mind that you don't have to be a hero. You don't have to change your lifestyle overnight. By simply just adopting some sort of exercise routine, you can well be on your way to better self-care. This can then enable you to have the emotional control you need to give the other people in your relationships the care that they need.

Self-care also involves understanding that you have your own needs. This means you have to reconnect with your values and your personal priorities.

Now, this sounds awesome in theory, but one of the simplest ways to do this is to simply take a break. Maybe you're in a toxic relationship and that needy person in your life wants you to be around constantly. It's as if they need you to hover over them on a 24/7 basis.

Well, according to a study published in 2003 by the *Journal for the Theory of Social Behavior*, when people take time out to be by themselves, they become happier.

I know it sounds crazy and it's unexpected because usually we define happiness in terms of sociability. In fact, some people are so social that they think they cannot be happy alone.

Well, psychologically speaking, it's actually the reverse. Maybe the reason why you're so unhappy and frustrated is because you're around that person who is so emotionally needy and you just need to solve this and exercise self-care. You just need to take a break.

The study showed that there is a big difference between being lonely and solitude. Solitude is a great way to refresh and recharge your spiritual intimacy, creative, and psychological batteries. This leads to better stress management, improved life satisfaction, and a lower tendency to suffer from depression.

Loneliness, on the other hand, is a mental state that can happen to people even if they're in a crowd. You can feel alone even when you're in a relationship. You can be in the arms of somebody and feel alone. So, don't confuse solitude with loneliness.

It's really important to take some time out because it's a great way of recharging your ability to communicate with people and also to give yourself the resources you need to provide the kind of care you've been providing to those who depend on you.

With all that said, self-care is easier said than done because, if you're codependent, you're not used to it. You might even think that it's very uncomfortable because you are taking time for yourself and it might even strike you as somehow selfish. But it's absolutely necessary if you want to take better care of other people.

Step by Step Guide to Self-Care

Step #1: Do a daily self-assessment

Simply ask yourself what you're feeling and what you think you need. One of the best ways to do this is to keep a journal and write down your reflections and your thoughts on a day to day basis.

Step #2: Try to do just one small thing that satisfies your needs daily

Again, as I've mentioned earlier, you don't have to be a hero. You don't have to jump into this with both feet and try to do everything all at once. A little bit of improvement on a day to day basis is enough.

For example, if you find yourself constantly tired taking care of everybody else's needs, you might want to just take a nap. It may seem simple, but pay close attention to the effect on your performance. It may turn out that you become more effective by simply taking care of yourself better.

If you see this pattern, then you can scale it up because now you know what the answer is. Now, it has become obvious to you that you can take care of yourself, and at the same time, become a better care provider to those around you.

Step #3: Adopt a daily stretching routine

By doing simple calisthenics on a day to day basis, you not only improve the flow of blood in your system as well as stretching your muscles, but this also sends signals to your nervous system, which can improve your overall spirit and mood.

By adopting a regular exercise program involving cardiovascular activities, you pump a lot more oxygen into your brain, and don't be surprised if you have a lot more energy and you're more patient throughout the day.

Step #4: Eat healthier

By eating less carbohydrates and loading up on protein and fat, you can manage your insulin cycles in such a way that your insulin peaks and crashes don't have to negatively impact your mood.

This can stabilize your mindset and lead to positive feedback loops which end up making you feel more confident, more alive, and in turn, more likely to take positive action.

This can then trigger another round of feeling good, and before you know it, you have better self-esteem, you become more confident, and you end up becoming a more effective person overall.

Step #5: Take the time to read a book

You may be thinking to yourself that reading a book is something very small and almost insignificant. Think again. When you read a book, you're automatically taking time away from the codependent person in your life.

This person is an emotional sponge and usually takes up a lot of your time. But when you read a book, you basically are saying, "This time that I'm taking to read a book is off limits. This is for me."

And when you read a book, you actually train your mind to do many things at once. At the most basic level, you are boosting your memory. Obviously, when you read a novel, for example, you're keeping track of the plotline.

In addition to this, when you read literature or a well-written novel, you actually get in the heads of other people. This can jumpstart how relationships should be or how other people think, and this enables you to gain some perspective.

There may be other truths out there, and by being reminded of this dynamic, you can start seeing your situation from a different perspective and this can change your mindset.

Chapter 9: Practice Self-Compassion

Let me be clear, if you practice compassion on yourself, you will break your codependency. This is the key.

But the reason why I put this in Chapter 8 or near the middle of the codependency tips I'm sharing in this book is that this requires quite a bit of a warm-up. Put simply, you can't use this as number one.

People who are caught in codependent patterns take a long time to get out of those patterns. Putting this front and center or as the initial step will take too much of their resources and could seem too much of an abrupt break and they don't end up making much progress.

Regardless, by the time you practice enough self-care and you've stopped denying that you have a problem as well as deciding and enforcing your personal boundaries, you will be ready for self-compassion.

In a study that appeared in the *Clinical Psychological Science Journal*, student participants who have self-compassion were able to show physiological signs of control even when put under stressful circumstances.

This study involved 135 students, divided into five groups. They were attached to all sorts of testing equipment to measure their heart rates and other physiological responses They were then given a questionnaire that measured their level of self-compassion as well as their connection to other people. They also were asked to describe how they felt.

Two groups of study participants were instructed to engage in self-compassion exercises. This took the form of a loving-kindness meditation or a body scan meditation.

Interestingly enough, of all the five groups, these participants reported the highest level of self-compassion, but they are also the ones with the more relaxed heart rate, reduced sweat response, and heart rate variability.

The researchers running the study made the note that heart rate variability actually plays a big role in how people respond to all sorts of stressful situations. In terms of their feedback to the questionnaires, the self-compassion people are less likely to criticize themselves.

Compare this with people who tended to look at themselves more critically. These are self-critical individuals who think they haven't really achieved much with their lives. When tested for physiological responses, they're more likely to show signs of stress.

The co-author of the test concludes that these findings show that using cognitive therapy can benefit people with recurrent bouts of depression. This ties in with codependency because people who find themselves caught in codependent patterns tend to have low esteem.

They feel that they don't deserve to be in a healthy relationship. They know that the person they're with has serious problems but their self-esteem is so low that they think they don't deserve to be happy. They don't deserve a better person.

And their partner uses this vulnerability to keep them stuck in the relationship. They're not happy, their partner is not happy, and it's a downward spiral from there.

Interestingly enough, self-compassion can help the codependent but non-addicted partner or non-impaired partner get through the rough periods in the relationship and overcome adversity long enough to possibly start the healing process. Again, this goes back to self-care.

If you were to choose to be the adult in your relationship, you can help turn things around by standing up for your rights, drawing boundaries, and eventually pushing your partner to mature. You're not helping him or her by enabling their addictive or self-destructive instincts or patterns.

Indeed, self-compassion is a good indicator of how well people can overcome potentially emotionally devastating events like divorce and marital separation.

In the journal *Psychological Science*, published in 2011, 105 subjects were interviewed and asked to talk about their former partner. The interviewees were screened in terms of their levels of self-compassion.

After the initial interview, the participants were asked to come back after three months, six months, and then nine months. They were then asked to report emotional issues that they may have had since the last time they walked in.

All told, people who had higher levels of self-compassion reported less incidents of hyper emotional arousal and emotional turbulence. In other words, people who went through a rough breakup and divorce are more likely to weather such emotionally turbulent times if they practice self-compassion.

Step by Step Guide to Practicing Self Compassion

Step #1: Allow yourself to be kind to yourself

It's easy to say that you're kind to yourself. Anybody can say that. But you actually have to deliver it.

How? You have to treat yourself the same way you would treat a friend who is going through a tough time. How would you comfort that person? What kind of words would you use? How would you approach that person?

Apply these to yourself.

Interestingly enough, when you do this, you feel better – the same way as your friend would better. By simply taking time to listen to yourself, you go a long way in helping your mental and emotional clouds to settle.

This takes quite a bit of patience. You also need to find the time to do this. You can't rush through this process, which brings me to Step #2.

Step #2: Practice mindfulness

There are many different flavors of mindfulness out there. You can look at an object intently for several minutes, taking all its details and moving slowly from detail to detail. When you do this, you free up a lot of your mental resources.

When you allow your mind to focus, this builds discipline. It also unclenches your mind from the things you normally worry about. You stop being regretful of past child sexual abuse, physical abuse, or whatever mental or emotional baggage you may be carrying.

This also frees you up from worrying about the future. Because let's face it, worrying about things that have not yet happened is just a complete and total waste of time.

When you just focus on something so basic as like a cup in front of you, or a table in front of you, you free up all that mental firepower and just focus on living in the present moment. This enables you to not only identify negative self-talk that you may engage in, but you start seeing negative beliefs you have about yourself.

We all have a narrative. We all have a background script that we tell ourselves. Maybe you say to yourself that you're an idiot, maybe you say to yourself that your parents don't love you or your brother is always better than you or you don't have any money and you're poor, you're a loser, or any other kind of negative self-talk.

When you practice mindfulness, these bubble to the surface because your mental focus is so centered on the here and now and the present moment that a lot of these become apparent and you're more likely to identify them and get them out of the way.

Step #3: Realize that your situation is not unique

If you've been trapped in a codependent relationship, it's very easy to think that all the burdens of the world are resting squarely on your shoulders. It's as if nobody is going through what you're going through. All that pain, confusion, doubt, or struggle you're feeling seems so vivid and so strong that it seems like you're going through this unique torture.

Well, I hate to break it to you, but you're not all that special. Whatever you are going through, somebody has gone through before. In fact, many people all over the world are going through something worse.

You may be in a codependent relationship, but did you know that in many countries, and also in many relationships, even in the same city as you, there's a lot of physical abuse? There's a lot of drug abuse? There's a lot of sexual abuse? So regardless of how harsh psychologically you think your situation is, it can be worse.

If you're able to break past that impasse, then it's much easier to realize the second conclusion that you need to wrap your mind around. The second conclusion is that it may seem that all these things are heavy, but you don't have to carry all the burdens of the world. You don't have to carry the responsibility for somebody's life.

Your father and mother, they may have made mistakes. Your brother might be an addict. Your lover might have serious problems. But ultimately, those are their problems.

You have no right bearing all these burdens because even if you were to bear all their sins and their screw ups, this doesn't necessarily mean that they will improve. In fact, in many cases, you give them permission to screw up even worse.

So, stop taking it all on. Relieve yourself of the burdens of other people and allow yourself to breathe. You've got enough problems of your own and you really have no business making things worse on yourself by assuming other people's issues.

If you exercised Step #2 correctly, this becomes easy because now you have boundaries. You can now say to yourself, "Well, this is mine and that is yours."

Just because your partner is screwing up, it doesn't necessarily mean that you have to go down the drain with them. It's okay to feel compassion, it's okay to feel bad, but ultimately, they have to be responsible for their lives just as you have to be responsible for your life.

Take ownership of your own life and, before you know it, they become more responsible.

The worst thing that can happen is to reduce your romantic partner into a child. Because the more you take up their problems, the less likely they are to grow.

Step #4: Give yourself enough room to be human

Nobody's perfect. You're a human being, and it's perfectly okay to realize that you're not perfect and you will never be perfect. So, if you can wrap your mind around these central facts, then realize that it's okay to screw up.

Of course, we don't want to screw up. We don't intentionally fail. But when they do happen, we don't have to allow them to crush us.

If you make the wrong decision, and believe me, nobody's immune from this, don't be too hard on yourself. Allow yourself to be human. Just because things didn't work out, it doesn't necessarily mean that you are a failure.

Don't define yourself by your pain. Don't define yourself by your loss or your mistakes. Instead, look at yourself as somebody who is incomplete, but who is learning. This is part of your journey.

Of course, this doesn't mean that you have to refuse responsibility for them or own up to them. Own that decision. You screwed up. You made the wrong turn. But instead of defining yourself based on the failure, see yourself as a learning organism that can benefit from this experience.

Step #5: Don't give up on the process

It's very easy to look at the whole process of overcoming codependency as an uphill battle. I mean, after all, this pattern has existed in your relationship for so long.

Your mother has been verbally abusive for so long. Your father has been emotionally absent for so long. Your brother can't seem to get his act together. Your girlfriend is addicted to drugs or whatever else. You may be thinking to yourself, "This is just impossible."

Well, the truth is, instead of looking at breaking codependency as some sort of problem, look at it as a challenge. These are two totally different things.

Because when you look at a challenge, you are looking at an opportunity to take the strengths that you have and look at the person who you think you are and step up.

Heroes are made when they break and get back up and grow. That's how heroes grow. That's how people mature.

Life is supposed to be hard. Believe it or not, life is supposed to be unfair. Because if life was easy, then there would be no growth. That is the blessing of pain. That is the miracle behind loss.

So, you have to stop avoiding challenges and start embracing them and seeing the beauty in them.

I know this is counterintuitive, but believe me, if you are in the pit of codependency, chances are, you tried to do what you normally do, which is to run to pleasure and stay away from pain.

How has it been working out for you? If you're reading this book, I would like to make a bet that it hasn't been going well.

So instead of running away from the "problems," start looking at them in a different light. Sure, that person you're codependent to may look like they don't want to change. Maybe they're abusive, maybe they're manipulative – but instead of brooding and nursing this resentment against them, look at the situation you're in as a challenge.

Train your inexhaustible imagination and resourcefulness to this problem set. Take one step at a time. Don't expect yourself to solve it overnight.

Instead of criticizing yourself and comparing yourself constantly to other people, your family members, or constantly beating yourself up by calling yourself an idiot or a loser, embrace the challenge. Say to yourself that "I can solve this. I have the resources and I can learn."

So, at the very least, draw inspiration from survivors of codependent relationships who have managed to turn their relationship around and grow. At the very least, look at the people who have successfully found themselves out of such codependent relationships.

Remember, there are certain cases where you just have to cut the person off. If you are in a codependent relationship with a drug addict and that person just doesn't want to change, the best thing you can do for that person is to cut that person off. That's how you can grow. That's how you can give them the space to hopefully realize their need for growth. Don't give up on the process.

Chapter 10: Build a Strong Support System

People in codependent relationships persist longer in such hurtful and unproductive situations precisely because they're isolated.

If they have kept in touch with other people in their lives or they have kept in touch with their network of friends, there's a good chance that honest people could tell them what's going on and possibly help them find their way out of that codependency. Maybe they can get inspired to do what they need to do to possibly heal their relationship.

The problem is, in a codependent relationship, eventually, both partners become isolated. This is especially true when it comes to abuse.

If your partner is beating you up, slapping you around and your bruises give away the physical abuse in your relationship, it's not uncommon for you yourself to shy away from other people. Since it's obvious that your partner is smacking you around, you feel ashamed.

Also, you want to protect your partner because you don't want him or her to go to jail. So, you cut yourself off, and this can lead to a downward spiral of mental and emotional isolation.

This is what makes the codependency worse. At first, it's just a very tough spot to be in, but eventually, it becomes some sort of trap that you can't get out of.

In a May 2007 report in the journal *Psychiatry* published by the researcher, Edgemont, when people are in a social support network, these individuals are more likely to exhibit resiliency when exposed to stress. This report highlighted the effect on the hypothalamic pituitary adrenocortical or HPA system.

When we have a support network of friends and family members, it helps smooth our HPA system so that we physically are able to withstand a lot more of the psychological stresses we find ourselves in.

This is an interesting study because it showed that social networks has a physiological effect, which can then help people deal with emotional issues better.

Step by Step Guide to Building a Support Network

Step #1: Show yourself love by asking for help

This is a very important step. For a lot of people, it's nearly impossible. They think that it's an admission of failure when they feel that they have to ask for help regarding the codependency and emotional issues of their relationships. They think that this just highlights their weakness. I'm, of course, talking especially about men.

Well, believe it or not, when you ask others for help, this is one of the best ways you can love yourself. The bottom line is, you're not doing yourself any favors when you are feeling down in the dumps, overwhelmed, anxious, confused or lonely.

When you feel like you're drifting out there and there's nobody to reach out to because you didn't bother to create a support network, who do you think suffers? Not them, but you.

You have to break out of your pride. You have to overcome your notions of shame. Because the more you keep this private, the more cut off you become and it just gets worse and worse.

This is not an admission of failure or weakness. Instead, it is one of the best things you can do to yourself out of self-love.

Step #2: Learn to recognize and accept help from others

Believe it or not, even if you're not reaching out to other people, it may well turn out that they are already reaching out to you.

The problem with a lot of people who are caught up in codependent relationships is that they have become completely blind or partially blind to these offers of help.

You have to remember that people are sensitive to what you're going through and they're usually not going to be obvious about their offers for help. Still, just because these offers are subtle, it doesn't take away from the fact that they are still offers for help.

Do yourself a big favor and understand how this works and how to recognize offers of emotional and mental support.

People in a codependent relationship, especially those with controlling partners, are trained early on to look at such emotional outreach from family members and friends as some sort of meddling. They think that these people are stepping into their personal lives and bossing them around. Well, you need to overcome that programming.

You have to understand that, first and foremost, when people are reaching out to you, they're doing so because they want to help you. They're not doing it because they want to run your life or because they feel that they know better than you. Instead, they're trying to help you. If you're able to bring yourself to this, then progress is possible.

Step #3: Surround yourself with the right people

This is tricky. Usually, when we think of nurturing and helpful people, it's very easy to imagine these people as basically soothing us all the time. They seem to say the right words and the right time that make our problems easier to bear.

If only life were that way. If only reality was that way.

Oftentimes, the best friend you could ever need is somebody who would tell it to you straight. This is somebody who would keep it 100.

Here's the problem. Most people, especially those who are caught in the negative feedback loop and addictive patterns of codependency, don't want to hear the truth.

If you're an addict, the last thing you want to hear from somebody is them calling you an addict. That's the last thing that you want to hear. But let me tell you, that's the first thing you need to hear. Keep this is in mind.

Because surrounding yourself with the right people doesn't mean surrounding yourself with "yes" people. These are people who are always saying "yes" to you or are ready, willing and eager to come up with all sorts of excuses and justifications to explain away your negative behavior.

You don't need those people because they're not doing you any good. If that's how you define support, then it's very easy for you to stay in your abusive relationship and not make any progress because these people will come up with all sorts of reasons why things are okay.

That's not the kind of help you need. Instead, you need somebody who will call a spade a spade. Now, you might hate that person, you might think that this person has it in for you, but this person's truth is exactly what you need.

You have to understand that codependent relationships thrive on lies. Your partner lies to you and you lie to your partner. And one lie leads to another and it starts a self-reinforcing process and both of you eventually become blind to the truth.

If you are lucky enough to have a friend who calls things the way they are, then you will be blessed indeed.

It may be painful at first. After all, who likes being called an addict or an enabler? But eventually, you would realize that this person is saying the truth and this is exactly what you need.

And when you report back to that person regarding the hard actions you've taken, this person is not going to mince words. This person is not going to say, "Well, that's good enough. Carry on." No. This person will say, "Step it up. Take it to the next level. Keep pushing forward."

Because you have to understand that we know that we are dealing with the truth when we are faced with realizations that are not all that comfortable. In fact, in many cases, you know you're dealing with the truth when it hurts. Because when you feel that hurt, part of you is dying.

This is good news because this may be the part of you that is in that codependent relationship. It's that part of you that just refuses to grow up and face reality.

Let that person die. Let that person hurt. Come out of that person.

Step #5: Stay away from negative people

Now, you're probably thinking to yourself, didn't I just repeat myself? Didn't I just say that there are certain people that will give you uncomfortable truths and you should hang out with these people? These people open your eyes to the reality that you often refuse to see. So, what does this have to do with staying away from negative people?

Well, you have to understand that people who spell out the truth in a loving way, motivated by nothing but love for you, are exactly the kind of people you need to stick around with. These are people who give you that steady diet of truth that you need to overcome your codependent relationship.

By negative people, I'm talking about people who are just unhappy. These are people who drain a lot of your emotional energies and give nothing back. These are people who enable you to feel even worse or who stoke your negative tendencies. You know who these people are.

For example, if you're talking about a female friend who both of you don't really like all that much, you know that this person is negative when she makes a big deal about the foibles and shortcomings that you initially raised, so she raises those issues. You agree, and then you raise other issues, and then she raises again, so before you know it, you're just feeding each other's negativity.

Stay away from those people because not only would they do that to people both of you don't like, who knows what she's doing when you have your back turned?

You have to stay away from negative and emotionally draining people. Instead, stick around people who will give you that fresh dose of truth and who have the moral and emotional inner strength to walk with you through this difficult process.

And the way to do this is to always view this seemingly negative bombardment of facts as a form of self-love. You say to yourself, "I'm hanging out with this person, as painful as these truths may be, because I love myself that much." And before you know it, everything will fall into place.

Chapter 11: Seek Professional Help

There are certain situations in any kind of codependent relationship where professional medical help is required. In many cases, codependency can be treated on a self-help basis.

For example, if you are codependent primarily because of your attitude and your mindset, chances are, there's a lot you can do on your end to turn things around.

You don't necessarily have to take psychotherapeutic medication. You don't have to take Prozac or anti-anxiety drugs like Paxil. You can simply monitor how you respond to certain stimuli and engage in cognitive behavioral therapy to overcome.

However, if you are diagnosed as being medically or clinically depressed, that's another story altogether. This doesn't mean that there is absolutely no space for cognitive behavioral therapy in that situation. Instead, what this should tell you is that all your self-help efforts should be undertaken under the direct supervision of a qualified medical professional.

Whether that person is a licensed social worker, a licensed psychologist, or a psychiatrist, it doesn't really matter. Get the right help if you are clinically diagnosed or if you are already taking medication for a related condition like anxiety or depression.

The Usefulness of Talk Therapy

It's tempting to think that once you are subject to the supervision of a qualified medical professional for your codependency that you're basically stuck with drugs. This is not true.

One of the most effective ways to overcome codependency is through talk therapy. Basically, the licensed professional will go through certain scenarios with you and help you pick apart how you look at certain traumatic events or facts in your life. It may well turn out that you're just interpreting these in a counterproductive way.

With enough expert guidance and certain exercises, eventually, you can start to change how you look at these situations and facts and end up with different mental and emotional states.

This can then lead to different actions, which can create positive feedback loops. You act differently, which leads to you feeling differently, which then strengthens further positive action.

Please understand that just as codependent relationships often involve downward spirals where one partner is mentally impaired or emotionally damaged, and this leads to a codependent response from the other partner, which then makes their behavior worse, which then leads to worse feelings, and down and down it goes.

This can also be flipped. That's right. It can go easily the other way.

When you make progress in your relationship and that person is responsive, it makes you feel better. And you not only feel better about yourself, but you feel better about the relationship, and this enables you to act in a more positive way, which then encourages that person to act and behave more positively, and on and on it goes. It's an upward spiral.

And the good news is that you have a lot more control about the direction this feedback loop takes in your relationship. Just because your partner slaps you around or abuses drugs, it doesn't mean that that's the end of the relationship. That doesn't mean that this is all there is to your relationship with that person or your parent. You have a lot more control over the process than you give yourself credit for.

Conclusion

Please understand that codependent relationships differ from relationship to relationship. This is the absolute truth.

How come? Well, the bedrock problematic behavior in one relationship that forms the dependency varies from relationship to relationship.

For example, in one relationship, one partner may be addicted to porn. In another relationship, the other partner is addicted to drugs. In another relationship, the other person is the product of child sexual abuse. In another relationship, that person is a survivor of horrific physical abuse.

Obviously, these are different from each other. Also, the coping mechanisms of both partners change based on the underlying experience of each partner.

So, don't think that there's some sort of magical one-size-fits-all formula for curing any and all codependency. No such animal exists.

Instead, you have to look at your specific codependent relationship based on its merits and based on its facts. This way, you can come up with a coping mechanism that would be equally useful to you and your partner.

The first step is to decide that there is a problem. You cannot wait for your partner to get his or her act together.

If you decide to play that game, you're probably going to wait forever. In fact, it's probably much better for you to just break up with that person because tomorrow is never going to come. They or you will always come up with some sort of excuse or justification why you have to kick the can down the road.

Stop playing these games with yourself. Stop waiting for tomorrow. If your relationship is going to get healed and if you are going to live a happier and more fulfilled life, it has to start today.

Don't be afraid to focus on yourself. I know, if you're a codependent person, you're probably thinking that the other person is dependent on you.

Maybe you are caring for a parent, or maybe you are caring for a father with dementia or Alzheimer's. In that situation, it's very tempting to think that you cannot take care of yourself first because this is selfish. After all, that person in my life is suffering. He needs me.

Well, by focusing on your healing first, you would be in a better position to help them heal. Because if you continue to be damaged, they're never going to heal.

They are always going to remain addicted. They are always going to remain damaged. They are always going to perpetuate the pattern that they've grown accustomed to. In other words, you have to choose to be the adult in your relationship.

This is how healing starts. And it begins by you taking action on yourself.

Believe it or not, once your family member, partner or friend sees you change because you have started taking better care of yourself, they get encouraged. They see for themselves that there is a way out of this pit that they're in. It doesn't have to be some sort of death trap. It doesn't have to be hopeless.

Be that ray of light. And while it will involve some touchy and even painful interactions with them, once they see that you make enough progress in the path of healing, they would see that this is a gamble worth taking.

I know that the road to codependency recovery is rough. It has a lot of twists and turns. But it's definitely a road you need to take. I wish you nothing but the best.

Copyright © 2019 by Nick Anderson

All rights reserved. No part of this book may be reproduced in any form without permission in writing from the author.

No part of this publication may be reproduced or transmitted in any form or by any means, mechanical or electronic, including photocopying or recording, or by any information storage and retrieval system, or transmitted by email or by any other means whatsoever without permission in writing from the author.

DISCLAIMER

While all attempts have been made to verify the information provided in this publication, the author does not assume any responsibility for errors, omissions, or contrary interpretations of the subject matter herein.

The views expressed are those of the author alone and should not be taken as expert instruction or commands. The reader is responsible for his or her own actions.
The author makes no representations or warranties with respect to the accuracy or completeness of the contents of this work and specifically disclaims all warranties, including without limitation warranties of fitness for a particular purpose. No warranty may be created or

extended by sales or promotional materials. The advice and recipes contained herein may not be suitable for everyone. This work is sold with the understanding that the author is not engaged in rendering medical, legal or other professional advice or services. If professional assistance is required, the services of a competent professional person should be sought. The author shall not be liable for damages arising here from. The fact that an individual, organization of website is referred to in this work as a citation and/or potential source of further information does not mean that the author endorses the information the individual, organization to website may provide or recommendations they/it may make. Further, readers should be aware that Internet websites listed in this work might have changed or disappeared between when this work was written and when it is read.

Adherence to all applicable laws and regulations, including international, federal, state, and local governing professional licensing, business practices, advertising, and all other aspects of doing business in any jurisdiction in the world is the sole responsibility of the purchaser or reader.

Made in the USA
Las Vegas, NV
26 March 2024

87801038R00075